THE PSYCHOLOGY OF HABITS

How thinking patterns influence behaviour and habit formation

Grace Hopefield

Copyright © 2025 Grace Hopefield

All rights reserved

The characters and events portrayed in this book are fictitious. Any similarity to real persons, living or dead, is coincidental and not intended by the author.

No part of this book may be reproduced, or stored in a retrieval system, or transmitted in any form or by any means, electronic, mechanical, photocopying, recording, or otherwise, without express written permission of the publisher.

ISBN-9798308834267

Cover design by: Art Painter
Library of Congress Control Number: 2018675309
Printed in the United States of America

CONTENTS

Title Page
Copyright
Understanding Habits 1
The Science of Behavior Change 5
Cognitive Patterns Influencing Habits 9
Motivation and Habits 13
The Habit Loop 17
Building Positive Habits 20
Overcoming Procrastination 24
Environmental Influences on Habits 28
The Role of Emotions in Habits 31
Maintaining Habits Over Time 35
Habit Change and Identity 39
The Influence of Technology on Habits 43
Social Support and Habit Formation 47
Advanced Techniques for Habit Change 51
Reflection and Continuous Improvement 55
The Role of Psychology in Habits 59
The Power of Thinking Patterns 63
Identifying Your Habits 68
The Cycle of Change 72

Building New Habits	76
The Influence of Environment on Habits	80
Overcoming Barriers to Change	84
The Role of Mindfulness in Habit Formation	88
Technology and Habits	92
Motivation: Intrinsic vs. Extrinsic	96
Habit Formation in Different Life Stages	101
The Impact of Stress on Habits	105
The Future of Habit Research	109
Practical Steps for Lasting Change	113

UNDERSTANDING HABITS

Defining Habits: The Basics
A habit is a routine behaviour that is repeated regularly, often unconsciously. It can be as simple as brushing your teeth each morning or as complex as a workout regimen. Understanding habits involves recognizing their structure, typically consisting of a cue, a routine, and a reward. Some automatic habits operate in the background of our lives, often without our awareness, and even deliberate habits that require conscious effort. Moreover, habits can be grouped into different categories: health habits, productivity habits, social habits, and emotional habits, each serving distinct purposes in our lives. For example, health habits contribute to our physical well-being, while productivity habits enhance efficiency and management of time. Recognizing the various habits we form can help us identify which are beneficial and which might need re-evaluation.Habits are essential for daily functioning because they provide a structure that allows us to navigate our lives efficiently. When we engage in habitual behaviours, we conserve cognitive resources, enabling us to focus our mental energy on more demanding tasks. This is particularly important in a world filled with distractions and information overload. Habits also contribute to our sense of identity; they reflect our values and priorities, shaping how we see ourselves, and others perceive us. The routines we establish can help reduce decision fatigue, leading to better outcomes in both personal and professional settings. Furthermore, positive habits can improve

mental health and resilience, allowing us to manage stress more effectively while promoting a feeling of accomplishment and control.One practical approach to developing beneficial habits involves habit stacking. This technique involves attaching a new habit to an existing one. For example, if you want to introduce a daily reading habit, you could stack it onto your morning coffee ritual. Pairing the new behaviour with an established one creates a seamless transition, making it easier for your brain to adopt the change. Visual cues can also serve as reminders, enhancing your commitment to the new behaviour until it becomes second nature.

The Psychology Behind Habit Formation
Various psychological frameworks can help us understand the formation of habits, including Charles Duhigg's cue-routine-reward loop. This loop begins with a cue that triggers the behaviour, followed by the routine itself, and concludes with a reward that reinforces the habit. Understanding this structure helps individuals recognize the environmental cues that lead to habitual behaviour. Behavioural psychology also emphasizes operant conditioning, where actions are strengthened by reinforcement or weakened by punishment. Positive outcomes can effectively encourage repeating specific behaviours, which can form constructive habits.The cognitive processes involved in habit development often start with decision-making. Initially, an individual may consciously decide to engage in a new behaviour. Over time, however, this behaviour can become automatic as it is repeated consistently. This transition underscores the brain's ability to optimize efficiency through neural pathways. These pathways strengthen the more a behaviour is performed, allowing mental resources to be conserved for other tasks.Attention, motivation, and memory also play vital roles in this process. Focusing on the desired behaviour and finding intrinsic motivation can facilitate habit development. Engaging with the habit consistently and looped rewards helps reinforce these cognitive pathways, further embedding the habit into daily life.As

you consider how to incorporate new habits, reflect on your existing routines and identify the cues that trigger them. Starting with slight, manageable changes can prevent overwhelming feelings and increase your chances of success. Reinforcing these changes with immediate rewards can also motivate you to maintain them long-term. The journey of habit formation is gradual, so practice patience with yourself as you work toward more significant behavioural changes.

The Role of Context in Habit Development
Environmental factors play a crucial role in habit formation. The spaces we inhabit, the people we interact with, and even the time of day can significantly influence our behaviours. For instance, if you want to develop a habit of exercising regularly, your environment needs to support that objective. This can mean setting up a workout space at home, surrounding yourself with fitness-focused friends, or choosing a gym that fits comfortably into your routine. Distinct environments can trigger specific behaviours; this association between place and routine is essential to habit formation. Researchers have found that subtle changes in our surroundings, such as moving furniture or altering scenery, can disrupt good and evil existing habits. Thus, for anyone seeking to build new habits, it's vital to design an environment that fosters desired behaviours consciously.The significance of context extends beyond habit formation to their maintenance and modification. Circumstances change, and as they do, so may our relationships with our habits. For instance, if you successfully establish a morning routine centred on mindfulness, changing your work schedule can make that practice challenging. This shift necessitates a reevaluation of your context. It may require you to identify a new time of day that could work just as effectively or find alternative ways to maintain the essence of your morning practices. Knowing the context in which habits are formed and sustained can empower individuals to create more resilient routines. Flexibility becomes key; the ability to adapt and tweak habits according to one's environment ensures long-

term success. Whenever you sense a change in your habits, take a moment to analyze the context influencing these shifts. Adapting to your surroundings while keeping your core motivations intact can lead to more incredible personal growth.To optimize habit development in your life, consider performing a simple exercise: identify one current habit you wish to change or create. Analyze your environment and assess how it supports or hinders this habit. Look for potential modifications you could implement—whether that involves adjusting your workspace, altering a social circle, or establishing a more conducive timeline for your efforts. These environmental adjustments can support successful habit implementation and maintenance, guiding you toward lasting change.

THE SCIENCE OF BEHAVIOR CHANGE

How Behavior is Measured

Understanding how to measure behaviour is crucial for anyone interested in psychology. Various methods can quantify behavioural changes, each with its strengths and weaknesses. Observation is one common approach, allowing researchers to see how individuals interact in specific situations directly. This can be structured or unstructured, depending on the research goals. Another method is self-reporting, where individuals provide insights about their behaviours through surveys or interviews. Though self-reports can be subjective, they give valuable qualitative data that can highlight personal perceptions of change. Additionally, objective measures such as frequency counts of specific behaviours or physiological assessments, like heart rate or brain activity, can also indicate behavioural shifts. Combining these methods often yields a more comprehensive view of behaviour change, offering a richer dataset for analysis.Identifying indicators of effective behaviour change is equally important. Key indicators can be both qualitative and quantitative. For example, increased compliance with recommended behaviours, such as attending therapy or following a treatment plan, is a clear sign of progress. Changes in thought patterns, evident through improved self-talk or emotional responses, also serve as indicators. Furthermore, shifts in social interactions—such as increased social engagement or relationship improvements—can signify positive changes. Tools like behavioural assessments can help track these indicators over time, making it easier to measure progress. It's crucial to tailor measurements and indicators to fit specific behavioural goals, ensuring that progress can be accurately assessed and tangible outcomes can be achieved.Create a structured plan for effective measurement that outlines what behaviours you want to track and why. Review this plan regularly to ensure your methods yield meaningful data that can guide further action.

The Stages of Change Model

The Stages of Change Model, developed by Prochaska and DiClemente, outlines the journey individuals embark on when they seek to alter their behaviours. This model identifies five core stages: pre-contemplation, contemplation, preparation, action, and maintenance. Understanding these stages is crucial. In the pre-contemplation stage, individuals are often unaware of their need to change. They may resist thinking about problems or dismiss them as unimportant. A growing awareness of the desire for change exists in the contemplation stage. People begin to recognize the consequences of their behaviour, though they may still feel ambivalent or stuck in indecision. As they transition to preparation, they plan for change, setting small, actionable steps to take. In the action stage, individuals implement their plans, making significant shifts in behaviour. Finally, the maintenance stage involves an ongoing effort to sustain the changes achieved and prevent relapse into previous habits.Effective strategies vary depending on the stage of change an individual is experiencing. For those in the pre-contemplation stage, it may be beneficial to provide information and raise awareness about the benefits of change without pushing too hard, allowing them to consider their situation at their own pace. In contemplation, encouraging self-reflection through guided discussions or journals can help clarify feelings and motivations for change. When individuals reach the preparation stage, they can benefit from creating a structured plan and setting specific and achievable goals. During the action phase, strategies such as support groups or accountability partners can keep them motivated and focused on their objectives. Lastly, in the maintenance stage, reinforcing new habits through continued education and self-monitoring is crucial, as this helps prevent relapse and reinforces long-term commitment to change.Understanding these stages provides a clearer perspective on individuals' journeys and invaluable insight for psychologists and practitioners working to facilitate behaviour change. The key takeaway is that change is not linear; setbacks are part of the process. Individuals should be encouraged to approach this journey with patience and commitment, recognizing that every small step counts. By embracing this model, anyone looking to make a positive change can navigate their path with greater ease and understanding.

Neuroplasticity and Habit Change
The brain has an incredible capacity to reorganize itself, crucial in changing our habits. Neuroplasticity, the brain's ability to form new connections and pathways in response to experiences, underpins the habit change process. Specific neural circuits repeatedly activate when a habit is formed, solidifying those pathways. However, neuroplasticity weakens those circuits when we consciously decide to change a habit. Each time we make a different choice—perhaps opting for a healthier snack instead of a sugary one—our brain is reshaping itself. Over time, these new experiences create alternate pathways that can become as strong, if not stronger, than the old ones. This process doesn't happen overnight; it requires consistent effort and repetition. The more we practice making a new choice, the easier it becomes, and eventually, the new behaviour can become the default reaction.Understanding the relationship between neuroplasticity and learning new behaviours is fundamental for anyone interested in self-improvement. When we learn something new, whether a skill or a behaviour, our brain physically changes; new synapses are formed, and existing ones can be strengthened. Learning and habit formation share a lot of common ground, as both rely on the dynamic nature of the brain. To successfully

adopt a new behaviour, it often helps to break it down into manageable steps. For instance, if someone wants to incorporate more exercise into their daily routine, they might start with short walks and gradually increase the distance and frequency. As they engage in this new behaviour, their brain will adapt, reinforcing the connections associated with exercise. Techniques such as visualization or mindfulness can further enhance this process, helping embed the new habit into their daily lives.Regular practice and patience are key in leveraging neuroplasticity for habit change. Consider applying the principle of habit stacking, where you attach a new habit to an existing one. This makes it easier to remember and integrates it more seamlessly into your routine. For example, if you already make coffee in the morning, add five minutes while waiting for it to brew. By linking the two actions, you can facilitate change effectively. Over time, these minor adjustments can lead to significant transformations, demonstrating how the brain's remarkable ability to adapt and reorganize can empower us to reshape our habits and ultimately enhance our lives.

COGNITIVE PATTERNS INFLUENCING HABITS

Identifying Cognitive Distortions
Recognizing cognitive distortions is crucial for anyone trying to form better habits. These mental traps can sabotage our efforts without us even realizing it. One common distortion is all-or-nothing thinking, where you may see things as black and white, assuming that if you can't do something perfectly, it's not worth doing at all. This thinking can lead to frustration and discouragement, particularly when creating new habits. Another prevalent distortion is catastrophizing, where you envision the worst possible outcomes. This can make starting something new feel overwhelming, preventing you from taking the first step. Identifying these thinking patterns helps develop awareness and combat them effectively, setting the stage for healthier habits.Cognitive distortions significantly influence daily choices and behaviours. When you fall into the trap of discounting the positive, you may downplay any progress you make, leading to a cycle of negativity that can stall your growth. For example, if you implement a new exercise routine and feel great about it one day but then dismiss that feeling because you skipped a workout the next day, you're reinforcing a negative narrative. This way of thinking can result in a lack of motivation and even cause you to abandon your goals entirely. Moreover, emotional reasoning, believing that your negative emotions reflect reality, can alter your decision-making. If you feel anxious about a new challenge, you might convince yourself you're incapable of handling it,

leading to avoidance instead of action. Understanding these distortions allows you to pause, reflect, and choose responses that align with your goals rather than reactive thoughts driven by fear or doubt.To combat cognitive distortions, practice reframing your thoughts actively. When you notice a negative belief cropping up, challenge it with evidence. Ask yourself if there's an alternative way to view the situation or if your feelings are misguiding you. Keeping a thought diary can also be beneficial, as jotting down your thoughts can help clarify patterns and allow you to re-evaluate them. Start recognizing when these distortions appear in your life. As you do, you'll cultivate a more constructive internal dialogue, paving the way for sustainable habits and healthier lifestyle choices.

The Impact of Self-Talk on Behavior
Understanding how positive and negative self-talk influences your habits is crucial for personal development. The messages we tell ourselves can profoundly shape our actions and decisions. When self-talk is positive, it encourages resilience and fosters a mindset geared towards success. For instance, people who regularly affirm their abilities tend to take risks and pursue goals, reinforcing hopeful behaviours and habits. On the contrary, negative self-talk can create a cycle of doubt and fear. If someone repeatedly says, "I can't do this," they may start avoiding challenges, leading to personal and professional growth stagnation. Recognizing your self-talk patterns can help you understand how they influence your daily choices and long-term habits, revealing the impact of your inner voice on your overall well-being.Identifying techniques to foster constructive self-dialogue is essential for cultivating better habits. Start by becoming aware of your thoughts by journaling your self-talk. Write down moments of self-doubt and instances of negative thoughts. Consciously challenging these perceptions is a crucial step. Replace harmful statements with healthier alternatives. For example, instead of thinking, "I'll never finish this project," shift to "I will do my best, and that's enough." Techniques such as

visualization can also be beneficial; imagine yourself succeeding and feel the confidence flow from that imagery. Additionally, practising mindfulness to stay grounded in the present can help reduce the frequency and intensity of negative self-dialogue. Building a positive internal narrative takes time, patience, and practice, but the rewards manifest in healthier habits and improved mental states.Lastly, a helpful tip is to create a self-affirmation mantra that resonates with you. Repeating phrases like "I am capable" or "I embrace challenges" can slowly rewire your thinking. Place reminders around your home or workspace or set prompts on your phone to reinforce this positive dialogue. This practice helps curb negative thoughts and strengthens your capacity for growth in every aspect of your life.

Techniques to Reframe Negative Thoughts

Shifting negative thinking patterns requires intentional effort and practical strategies. One effective method is identifying common cognitive distortions that often cloud your judgment. For instance, people frequently engage in all-or-nothing thinking, viewing situations in black-and-white terms without recognizing the grey areas. They might label the whole experience as a failure when a minor setback occurs. Instead, practice recognizing these distortions and consciously replacing them with more balanced thoughts. If you missed a workout, instead of thinking, "I'll never be fit," reframe it to, "I can get back on track tomorrow." Another strategy is to use humour to lighten your negative thoughts. When you are in a downward spiral, ask yourself how you would advise a friend in a similar situation. By viewing it from an outside perspective, you can often discover a more rational and humorous take on the issue. Additionally, mindfulness practices can significantly aid in reframing; being present allows you to detach from negative thoughts rather than engulf them. Regularly practising mindfulness can cultivate greater awareness of your thought patterns, making shifting your focus to more constructive narratives easier.Reframing is not just about changing thoughts; it is vital in enhancing your capacity for healthy habits. When you view challenges as opportunities for growth, you are more likely to engage in activities that benefit your well-being. For instance, if you perceive working out as a tedious chore, it's easy to skip sessions. However, if you reframe it as a joyful time for self-care or an opportunity to connect with friends, you may find it easier to commit. This positive perspective can create a ripple effect, encouraging you to develop and maintain healthy habits, such as proper nutrition and adequate sleep. Instead of labelling a nutritious meal as a restriction, consider it a nourishing and energizing choice that enhances your performance and mood. Each time you successfully reframe your thoughts in a positive direction, you improve your mindset and reinforce the actions aligned with your aspirations. To build this cycle, keep reminders of your goals visible. Whether it's a vision board or a simple sticky note, these cues can reinforce a positive mindset and help you stay focused on the beneficial habits you wish to cultivate.Reframing a routine part of your life can significantly influence your overall mental health. Whenever you notice negative thoughts surfacing, consciously take a moment to examine their validity. Challenge these thoughts and look for evidence that contradicts them. Remember, it is the practice that strengthens your ability to reframe. As you learn to work through negative thoughts with patience and intent, you will foster resilience against setbacks and in pursuing all areas of your life. One practical tip is to carry a small notebook where you jot down negative thoughts and immediately write reframed versions next to them. This simple act can transform your perception over time and improve your mental and emotional well-being.

MOTIVATION AND HABITS

Intrinsic vs. Extrinsic Motivation

Intrinsic motivation refers to doing something because it is inherently interesting or enjoyable. This type of motivation drives individuals to engage in activities purely for the pleasure or satisfaction of the activity. For example, a person who loves painting may spend hours working on a canvas simply because they enjoy the creative process. On the other hand, extrinsic motivation involves performing a task to earn rewards or avoid negative consequences. External rewards such as money, grades, praise, or trophies can strongly influence behaviour. While intrinsic and extrinsic motivations can effectively encourage specific actions, they stem from different sources, highlighting the importance of understanding how each can affect behaviour and decision-making.The impact of motivation on habit formation is significant. Intrinsic motivation often leads to longer-lasting habits because the individual engages with the activity out of genuine interest. When people derive joy or satisfaction from their actions, they are more likely to repeat those behaviours, naturally reinforcing the habit. Conversely, habits formed through extrinsic motivation may be less stable over time. While external rewards can initiate behaviour, the motivation to continue the behaviour might fade once those rewards are removed or diminished. This is evident in scenarios where individuals only work out to lose weight or earn a bonus, as opposed to those who enjoy physical activity and find it rewarding.Understanding the balance between intrinsic and extrinsic motivation can enhance personal goal achievement. Cultivating intrinsic motivation for tasks you wish to turn into lasting habits can help. Engaging in activities that excite you and align with your natural interests can help sustain your commitment over time. Consider setting personal challenges or milestones that highlight the activity's joy rather than focusing on external rewards. Even when external incentives are involved, connecting them to your interests can deepen your engagement and strengthen your habits in the long run.

The Role of Goals in Habit Formation
Setting specific and measurable goals plays a crucial role in creating new habits. When goals are well-defined, they provide clear direction and motivation, making it easier to carve out routines supporting them. For instance, instead of saying, I want to get fit, a more specific goal is to exercise for 30 minutes five days a week. This clarity helps individuals understand exactly what steps to take and encourages consistency. The more precise you are, the more your brain can engage with your goal and the habit formation process. Measurable goals allow you to track progress, celebrate small victories, and adjust your approach if necessary, fostering a cycle of motivation essential for long-term habit development.Aligning your goals with your desired habits requires intentionality and reflection. Start by identifying the habits you want to establish. For example, if your goal is to maintain a healthy diet, consider the habits that support this aim, such as meal prepping on Sundays or choosing fruits over sweets. CreatingIt's a plan that connects these habits to your broader objectives is essential. Establishing triggers can also help; specific times, locations, or events remind you to engage in your desired habits. Setting milestones within your goals can keep you engaged and accountable, ensuring that you pursue the end goal and the process of building sustainable habits.Lastly, remember that habit formation is not a one-time event but a process requiring ongoing effort. Regularly revisiting and refining

your goals keeps them relevant and aligned with your current aspirations. This adaptability is key to sustaining habits over the long run. Even minor adjustments can reignite your enthusiasm and commitment. Utilize tools like journals or habit-tracking apps to monitor your progress and stay committed. The next time you find yourself struggling with a habit, take a moment to reevaluate your goals and ensure they align with the changes you wish to make. This connection between goals and habits is vital—being intentional about this relationship can help facilitate lasting positive change.

Building Sustainable Motivation
Maintaining motivation over the long term can feel daunting, yet there are effective techniques to keep that drive strong. One powerful approach is to set clear, meaningful goals that resonate with your values. When goals are significant to you, they naturally fuel your motivation. Breaking these larger objectives into smaller, manageable tasks can create a sense of accomplishment and encourage a steady trajectory forward. It's also helpful to track your progress regularly, as this provides tangible evidence of your efforts and reinforces your commitment to your goals. Surrounding yourself with supportive peers and mentors creates a positive and motivational environment where ideas can thrive. Engaging with similar aspirations can inspire you to keep pushing your limits. Incorporating routines that promote well-being, such as exercise and mindfulness, can dramatically influence your mental state. These practices enhance self-awareness and resilience, ultimately making it easier to remain motivated in the face of obstacles.Reviving motivation during challenging times requires a proactive and reflective approach. When faced with setbacks, it's essential first to understand the underlying reasons for the dip in motivation. Taking a step back and identifying possible triggers—external stressors or internal doubts—can help address the root cause. Reassessing your goals during challenging periods also allows for recalibration. Sometimes, our aspirations must shift or adapt to

align with our current capabilities and circumstances. Embracing small victories can reignite your passion; celebrate even the tiniest accomplishments to build momentum. Additionally, consider revisiting your original inspirations. Reflecting on what initially sparked your motivation can remind you of your purpose and reignite that flame. One might also benefit from a temporary change of scenery or routine; a new environment can provide fresh perspectives and renewed energy to tackle challenges head-on. Staying adaptable is key to sustaining motivation in the long run. Often, it's about learning to flow with life's ebbs and flows rather than resisting them. Practising gratitude can shift focus from what isn't working to what is, creating a positive feedback loop that encourages progress. Remember that motivation is not constant; it fluctuates, which is perfectly normal. Recognize that periods of lower motivation can lead to introspection and growth if approached constructively. Ultimately, prioritizing self-care and being kind to yourself through these fluctuations can foster a more sustainable relationship with your motivation. Whenever you find yourself in a motivational slump, take a moment to reconnect with your vision. Visualizing your success can be a powerful motivator, so picture yourself achieving your goals and the feelings accompanying that vision. This practice can catalyze action, fueling your drive to progress despite hurdles.

THE HABIT LOOP

Cue, Routine, Reward: Understanding the Loop

The habit loop consists of three essential components: cue, routine, and reward. The cue is a trigger that initiates the behaviour, often occurring without conscious thought. It can be something external, like a time of day, a specific location, or even an emotional state. The routine is the behaviour, the action taken in response to the cue. Finally, the reward is the positive reinforcement that follows the routine, which helps establish a connection in the brain between the cue and the behaviour. This trio works together in a cycle that shapes habits over time.To leverage the habit loop for behaviour change, identify the existing cues that trigger unwanted routines. Self-reflection is key; consider your daily patterns and moments when you engage in behaviours you wish to alter. After identifying these cues, you can experiment with changing your routine. Choose a different reaction to the cue that aligns with your desired behaviour. This process often requires creativity and experimentation, as finding a substitute routine that still provides a rewarding experience is essential.

Breaking Down Daily Routines

Analyzing your current routines is a vital first step in understanding the balance between good and bad habits. Take a moment to observe what you do daily, consciously and unconsciously. Notice the small actions that fill your day, from when you wake up to when you sleep. Reflect on your morning rituals: Do you wake up and immediately check your phone, or do you take a few moments for mindful breathing? Think about how you navigate your workday. Are you prone to distractions, like scrolling through social media, or do you find yourself immersed in productive moments? By journaling these observations, you help clarify patterns that may serve you well or hinder your growth. Good habits, like dedicating time for self-care or setting aside moments for learning, can significantly boost your mental health. Conversely, bad habits like procrastination or mindless eating can detract from your overall well-being.Once you have identified these patterns, exploring techniques to disrupt harmful routines becomes essential. Consider employing the method of mindfulness to create a gap between your impulse to engage in an unhealthy habit and your response to it. For example, take a three-minute pause when you feel the urge to scroll on your phone instead of focusing on a task. During this pause, breathe deeply and redirect your thoughts to your long-term goals. Another effective strategy is the process of habit stacking. This involves taking a good habit you already have and attaching a new behaviour to it. If you want to reduce excessive screen time, pair a few minutes of reading with your morning coffee ritual. Gradually replacing harmful routines with more constructive ones redefines your day and reshapes your mindset over time.Embracing the practice of self-reflection and mindfulness can lead to transformative changes in daily behaviour. Set aside a few minutes each evening to review how well you adhered to your desired routines. Ask yourself what worked, what didn't, and why. This reflective practice helps anchor your intentions and strengthens your resolve to improve. Remember, it's not about perfection but progress. Small, consistent changes can lead to significant shifts in your life over time. As you cultivate awareness around your habits, you pave the way for a more intentional and fulfilling daily routine.

How to Identify Triggers for Bad Habits
Recognizing the triggers that lead to undesirable habits is the first step in transforming your behaviour. Triggers can be anything

from environmental cues to emotional states that stimulate the urge to engage in a habit. Begin by observing your daily routines and noting the moments when you feel compelled to act on a bad habit. For instance, do you reach for a snack when bored or anxious? You may notice that certain social situations lead you to smoke or drink excessively. By keeping track of these occurrences, you can identify patterns that clearly illustrate the connections between your triggers and your habits.Once you have identified your triggers, the next step is implementing strategies to manage or eliminate these stimuli. Consider creating a more supportive environment by removing objects or cues associated with your bad habits. If you tend to binge-watch television after dinner, try changing your evening routine with a new activity like reading or taking a walk. This slight shift can disrupt the automatic responses you may have developed. Additionally, practice mindfulness techniques to enhance your awareness of your emotional triggers. When you feel the urge to indulge in a bad habit, take a moment to pause and reflect on what you are feeling and why. Understanding the underlying emotions can empower you to choose a healthier response instead of reverting to old patterns.Building a toolkit of coping strategies is crucial in managing your triggers. Engaging in physical activity, practising breathing exercises, or even starting a new hobby can help divert your attention away from the trigger. These alternatives not only serve as distractions but can also provide a sense of accomplishment that makes it easier to resist the urge to fulfil the habit. Change takes time and persistence, so celebrate the small victories along the way. By combining recognizing your triggers with practical strategies to deal with them, you pave the way for lasting change that can improve your life.

BUILDING POSITIVE HABITS

The Power of Small Habits
Small, manageable habits are the building blocks of lasting change. Often, people feel overwhelmed when attempting to make significant changes, whether in their health, productivity, or emotional well-being. However, focusing on small habits allows us to gradually integrate new behaviours into our daily routines without the pressure of drastic transformation. When repeated consistently, these small actions create a stable foundation from which more significant changes can emerge. For example, consider starting with a ten-minute walk instead of committing to an hour of exercise every day. This feels achievable, and once it's established, it can naturally lead to longer sessions or more intense workouts. The key lies in consistency; when we make small changes, we are likelier to stick with them, fostering a sense of accomplishment that fuels our motivation for more significant progress.As small habits accumulate, they can create significant life changes. This concept is often called the compound effect, where tiny actions accumulate over time to produce remarkable results. When a small habit becomes ingrained in our daily lives, it paves the way for secondary habits to form. For instance, that ten-minute walk can evolve into a commitment to exercise three times a week, which may also lead to healthier eating habits. Each small win builds confidence and encourages us to take on more significant challenges. Moreover, small habits have a ripple effect; as we improve one aspect of our

lives, we often find ourselves inspiring and uplifting those around us. Our journey can ignite a desire for change in our friends and family, creating a supportive environment that fosters more small habits, further amplifying positive outcomes.To harness the power of small habits in your life, consider incorporating them into your daily routine. Start by identifying one small change you can commit to for the next month. It could be drinking a glass of water first thing in the morning or dedicating five minutes to mindfulness before bed. Keep the bar low to ensure it feels achievable, and track your progress to visualize growth. Consistency is vital; celebrate even the most minor victories, as they reinforce your commitment. Over time, you will likely notice how these minor adjustments can substantially improve your physical health, mental well-being, and overall quality of life. Remember, every great transformation begins with the decision to take that first small step.

Creating Effective Habit Stacking
Habit stacking is a powerful strategy that leverages the momentum of existing habits to incorporate new behaviours into your daily routine. The essence of this concept lies in the idea of linking a new habit to one that you already perform regularly. For instance, if you have a strong morning habit of making coffee, you might use that time to practice mindfulness for a few minutes. This method reduces the friction of starting a new habit and creates a seamless flow in your daily activities, making it easier to adopt positive changes in your life. The brain thrives on patterns, so by stacking your habits effectively, you can create a powerful sequence that enhances your productivity and encourages positive reinforcement.Many examples of successful habit stacks can inspire your own implementation. One well-known stack is the gym bag stack, where you place your gym clothes beside your bed. This simple action prompts you to get dressed for the day and encourages you to hit the gym right after you get up. Another functional stack is reading while you wait, such as reading a few pages of a book during your morning

commute or while waiting for your coffee to brew. The moments you already spend doing routine tasks can be transformed into opportunities for growth and improvement with some creativity. Observing how others have successfully integrated habit stacking can provide you with ideas that resonate with your lifestyle. As you create your habit stacks, think about context and timing. Identify your habits consistently and consider what small actions could fit into those routines. Start with one or two stacks, monitor how they fit into your life, and adjust as needed. Remember to keep it simple and realistic; the goal is to make new habits feel effortless by using the habits you already have. This practical approach enhances efficiency and builds confidence as you experience incremental successes, laying the groundwork for even more significant changes. A helpful tip is to keep a journal to track your habit stacks. Recording your progress can provide motivation and insight into what's working and what needs adjustment.

The Importance of Consistency
Consistency is the bedrock of effective habit-building. When individuals engage in a behaviour repeatedly, they create neural pathways in their brains that make it easier to perform those actions over time. This repetition helps to solidify habits, allowing them to become automatic. Without consistency, goals can seem overwhelming and unattainable. For instance, someone looking to exercise regularly might find that sporadic workouts provide little to no benefit. However, if they commit to a routine, even if it starts small, their body adapts, and the habit becomes part of their daily life. Moreover, consistent behaviours build confidence, as small successes lead to a greater belief in one's ability to achieve larger goals. The psychological satisfaction from seeing progress reinforces the importance of sticking to a routine, transforming efforts into an ingrained part of identity, making it less likely for one to abandon these commitments. Individuals can start by breaking down their goals into manageable chunks to cultivate consistency in daily routines. Instead of aiming to

run five miles every day, one might begin with just ten minutes of walking or jogging. Setting clear, achievable targets allows for gradual progress, and as people meet these smaller goals, they build momentum. Another effective strategy is establishing specific cues or triggers that signal when to perform a habit. For example, leaving workout clothes by the door can remind you to exercise after work. Additionally, tracking progress can provide visual feedback that reinforces commitment. Journals, apps, or simple checklists can help individuals see how far they've come, promoting continued effort. Social accountability also plays a crucial role. Sharing goals with friends, joining community groups, or finding an accountability partner can motivate and encourage one to stay on track. As a practical tip, consider implementing the two-minute rule, which suggests starting any new habit with just two minutes of activity. This approach lowers the barrier to entry, making initiating any routine feel less daunting. For instance, wear gym clothes instead of a complete workout and stretch for two minutes. This small act can often lead to more extended engagement as the inertia of starting works in your favour. Over time, these two-minute segments can lead to a more substantial change, illustrating how small, consistent actions pave the way for lasting transformation.

OVERCOMING PROCRASTINATION

Understanding the Roots of Procrastination
Procrastination is often rooted in various psychological factors that mould our behaviour. Anxiety is a significant player in this equation; the fear of failure can lead to avoidance. When faced with a daunting task, feelings of self-doubt can swell, causing one to delay starting the work. Perfectionism also feeds into this cycle. Individuals who set unrealistically high standards for their performance often fear that their output will not meet these expectations, leading to paralysis in decision-making and execution. Moreover, decision fatigue can come into play, where the overwhelming number of choices becomes too burdensome, resulting in procrastination. This stems from an inherent desire to avoid discomfort—whether it is the stress of getting it done or facing potential criticism from others. Every individual harbours underlying beliefs about themselves and their capabilities, profoundly affecting their tendency to procrastinate. For instance, someone with a strong belief in their abilities may confront challenges head-on, while others who doubt their skills might defer action to protect themselves from feelings of inadequacy. These beliefs can shape the task approach and the emotional responses to failures and successes. Limiting beliefs, such as I am not good enough or I will never succeed, can create a mental landscape where procrastination flourishes. Additionally, past experiences can skew current perceptions; a history of negative feedback may cause someone to avoid

situations where they risk receiving more of it. Recognizing and addressing these beliefs can be instrumental in breaking the cycle of procrastination.To effectively combat procrastination, it's vital to implement strategies that tackle psychological factors and underlying beliefs. One practical tip is to adopt a methodical approach to tasks. Breaking larger projects into smaller, manageable steps can reduce feelings of overwhelm and anxiety. Creating deadlines for each step, even self-imposed ones, can incentivize completion. Furthermore, practice mindfulness to recognize anxious thoughts and judgments without acting on them. Challenging negative beliefs by questioning their validity and replacing them with positive affirmations can shift one's mindset. With continued practice of these strategies, one can develop a stronger sense of agency, gradually diminishing the grip of procrastination.

Strategies to Combat Procrastination
Procrastination often arises from fear, overwhelm, and lack of clarity. To tackle these procrastination behaviours, it's essential to identify actionable strategies that can significantly improve your daily productivity. Start by breaking tasks into smaller, manageable parts. When faced with a daunting project, dividing it into bite-sized segments can lessen the mental burden. Assign specific deadlines to each mini-task, creating a structured timeline to motivate you to complete them. Visualizing progress can also be a powerful tool; consider using a checklist or progress tracker to see your achievements as you complete each segment. Additionally, change your environment to minimize distractions. A dedicated workspace, free from interruptions, can help maintain focus and efficiency.Implementing techniques that boost productivity and accountability can further enhance your ability to overcome procrastination. Establishing a routine is crucial; consistency helps form habits that reduce the likelihood of putting things off. Integrate the Pomodoro Technique into your workflow—working for a set amount of time followed by short breaks prevents burnout and keeps your mind fresh.

Pair this with accountability systems. Share your goals and deadlines with a friend, colleague, or mentor; knowing someone is aware of your obligations can propel you to stay on track. Consider using project management tools that allow for tracking progress and deadlines. They can be constantly reminders of what needs to be accomplished, creating a sense of urgency and responsibility.Finally, remember that mindset is just as crucial as methodology. Reframe your thoughts around tasks by focusing on the positive outcomes rather than the effort required. Acknowledge small victories and be kind to yourself when facing setbacks. Creating a supportive internal dialogue can help ease the pressure associated with tasks. Whenever procrastination creeps in, ask yourself the most minor action you can take right now. Even a tiny step forward can create momentum, making it easier to keep moving.

The Role of Time Management in Habit Formation
Effective time management is a fundamental element in reshaping and reinforcing habits. When time is managed well, it creates a structure that allows consistent actions over time. This consistency is crucial for forming habits that stick. For instance, if you want to establish a daily reading habit, allocating a specific time each day to read will not only make it easier. Still, it will also signal your brain that this activity is essential. This regularity transforms what might seem like a chore into an integral part of your routine. As you meet these time-bound commitments, your brain recognizes the pattern, making it easier to continue engaging in that behaviour. The key here is the predictability of effective time management; it cultivates an environment where habits can flourish without the constant uncertainty that often hinders our progress.You can incorporate several specific tools into your daily routine to enhance your time management skills. Tools such as calendars, planners, and digital apps are designed to help you prioritize tasks and allocate time efficiently. For example, using a planner allows you to jot down tasks and encourages you to assign them specific time slots. This makes you more likely

to complete these tasks and form habits around them. Apps like Todoist or Trello can also serve as invaluable resources, allowing you to track your habits visually. The visual aspect engages your motivation and helps maintain focus on what needs to be done. Whether you prefer a physical planner or a digital app, the key is to find a tool that resonates with you and suits your lifestyle, ensuring that time management becomes a seamless part of your daily routine.Incorporating these time management techniques doesn't have to be overwhelming. Start by identifying one or two habits you want to develop and use a tool to help schedule them into your day. For example, if you aspire to exercise regularly, set aside a dedicated time in your calendar for workouts. Treating these time slots as appointments that can't be missed reinforces these habits' importance. Over time, with consistent practice, these activities will start to feel automatic, and the effort required to maintain them will diminish. Remember, the essence of habit formation lies in persistence and regularity, and with well-structured time management, you create an environment conducive to lasting change.

ENVIRONMENTAL INFLUENCES ON HABITS

The Impact of Social Environment

The social environment plays a significant role in shaping our habits and behaviours. The people we surround ourselves with can inspire us towards positive change or lead us down a path of negativity. For instance, if your circle comprises health-conscious individuals, you are more likely to adopt healthier eating habits and exercise regularly. Conversely, if your friends indulge in unhealthy lifestyles, their choices may negatively affect your habits without you even realizing it. Our social connections often create a ripple effect where attitudes, beliefs, and behaviours are continuously exchanged.This influence is not confined to physical habits alone. Those around us can also sway emotional well-being. A support system filled with positive, encouraging friends can foster resilience during tough times, while a toxic environment might exacerbate feelings of anxiety and stress. Recognizing this dynamic allows us to take control of our social interactions and, ultimately, our habits.Cultivating a supportive social network is essential for effective habit change. Start by evaluating your current relationships and their impact on your goals. Seek out individuals with similar ambitions, as this shared purpose can enhance motivation and accountability. Joining groups or clubs related to your interests can also help connect you with like-minded individuals who encourage your growth.

Designing Your Space to Promote Good Habits

Arranging your physical environment can play a significant role in fostering positive habits. When you create a space that aligns with your desired behaviours, you invite success. Start by identifying the habits you want to cultivate. For instance, position books within easy reach on a neatly arranged shelf or a side table if you want to read more. Ensure your reading nook is comfortable and inviting, with good lighting and a cosy chair. By making your environment conducive to the habits you wish to develop, you not only ease the mental load of decision-making but also create an automated pathway to better choices.Incorporating design elements that promote routine is also essential. Use colour and decor intentionally; for example, warm colours inspire energy, while cooler tones induce calm. Visual cues serve as reminders of your goals. If you want to exercise regularly, place your yoga mat in a visible spot or hang up your running shoes where you can see them daily. Minimizing distractions is equally essential in this process. Declutter your workspace to help maintain focus, and consider noise-cancelling features or materials that absorb sound if you're in a bustling environment. Using storage solutions to keep your space organized can also reduce the mental clutter that often leads to procrastination. By deliberately designing your surroundings, you can enhance your ability to adhere to the habits most important to you.Consider setting up your environment as a strategic ally in your pursuit of self-improvement. A small yet effective tip is establishing a default arrangement for everyday tasks. For example, if you want to develop a journaling habit, leave your journal and a pen on your pillow or next to your morning coffee setup. This simple act transforms the journal into a constant visual reminder, prompting you to engage daily. By embedding your intentions into the very fabric of your space, every object can serve as a nudge toward your goals.

Reducing Exposure to Negative Influences

Identifying negative environmental cues is essential for anyone looking to sustain positive habits. These cues can lurk in various aspects of daily life, such as disorganized spaces, excessive screen time, or even certain social circles. When your environment is cluttered, it can create a mental fog that undermines your focus and motivation. It is crucial to recognize these influences because they can subtly steer you away from your goals. For example, if you're trying to adopt a healthier lifestyle but you are surrounded by junk food and negative conversations about weight loss, it becomes harder to stick to your plan. By staying aware of these negative cues, you empower yourself to take the necessary steps to limit their impact.Creating action plans can effectively minimize exposure to these detrimental influences. Start by mapping out your daily environment and identifying the specific cues that disrupt your desired habits. For instance, if you notice that social media leads to procrastination or anxiety, consider setting specific times for usage or employing apps that limit screen time. If the clutter in your living space reduces your productivity, develop a decluttering schedule to tackle areas systematically, allowing your space to inspire rather than hinder you. In social situations, you can set boundaries by kindly declining invitations that lead to environments where negative influences thrive. You can significantly reduce exposures that detract from your habits by proactively assessing where your attention and time go.A practical tip to begin this process is to review your environment and habits weekly. Reflect on what influenced you positively and negatively throughout the week. Use this insight to adjust your surroundings and routines for the following week, creating a continual improvement cycle. This way, you can gradually build an environment that aligns with your goals, enabling you to thrive in every area of your life.

THE ROLE OF EMOTIONS IN HABITS

Recognizing Emotional Triggers
Emotions play a pivotal role in shaping our behaviour, often driving the formation of positive and negative habits. Good habits, such as regular exercise, might be triggered by feelings of joy or a sense of accomplishment. On the other hand, bad habits like overeating or excessive screen time can arise from feelings of stress, sadness, or even boredom. Understanding these emotional factors helps us recognize why we engage in certain behaviours. For instance, when you feel anxious, you might seek comfort food to soothe yourself. This response can become a habit, reinforcing a cycle where the emotional trigger leads to a habitual action that might provide temporary relief but could also have negative consequences over time. Recognizing the contrast between how different emotions can lead to varying habits empowers you to consciously create beneficial practices that enhance well-being.Self-awareness is key to identifying your emotional triggers. Start by paying attention to your feelings and reactions in different situations. Keeping a journal can be a helpful exercise. Write down specific instances when you felt powerful emotions and note how you responded. Did you lash out in anger, seek comfort in food, or dive into a project enthusiastically? This reflection is essential for developing greater self-awareness. By analyzing your emotional responses, you understand the patterns influencing your habits. Are there certain times of day when you feel more emotional? Perhaps particular events,

people, or environments trigger specific feelings. As you uncover these triggers, you can devise strategies to alter your reactions, ultimately allowing you to replace unhealthy habits with positive alternatives.Look for practical ways to modulate your emotional responses once you identify your triggers. If you notice that stress leads you to procrastinate on tasks, consider engaging in mindfulness techniques like deep breathing or meditation when you feel overwhelmed. Establishing a new routine with short breaks helps redirect your focus and energy toward productive habits instead of slipping into negative patterns. It's crucial to remember that acknowledging your emotional triggers is just the first step; taking conscious action based on that recognition paves the way toward lasting change. Always be gentle with yourself in this process, as understanding emotional triggers is an evolving journey.

Managing Stress to Prevent Bad Habits
Understanding the connection between stress and negative habit formation is crucial for anyone seeking a healthier lifestyle. Stress can act as a catalyst for impulsive behaviours and unhealthy choices. When under pressure, the brain often defaults to familiar patterns, frequently negative habits, such as overeating, smoking, or excessive screen time. This connection is rooted in the brain's reward system. When stressed, individuals often seek immediate relief, and harmful habits can feel rewarding in the short term despite their long-term drawbacks. Recognizing stress as a trigger for these behaviours is the first step toward breaking the cycle. By being aware of when stress drives you to your bad habits, you can start to take control of your responses instead of letting the stress dictate your actions.Exploring stress management techniques can significantly improve your habits. Practising mindfulness, for example, allows you to stay present and aware of your thoughts and feelings without judgment. This can help you recognize when stress is beginning to escalate and will enable you to implement coping strategies before you resort to harmful habits. Breathing exercises offer immediate relief; a few deep breaths can lower your

heart rate and create a calming effect. Another effective technique is physical activity. Engaging in regular exercise not only reduces stress but also releases endorphins, which are natural mood lifters. Even a brief walk can shift your mindset and help diffuse stress. Journaling is another helpful tool. Writing about your thoughts and feelings can help you process stress, making it easier to deal with. By incorporating these techniques, you can create a personal toolkit that manages stress and supports the formation of more positive habits.Becoming conscious of your stressors and understanding how they influence your behaviour opens the door to healthier choices. Start by tracking your stress levels and the habits that emerge when you feel overwhelmed. This awareness lets you pinpoint your triggers and develop adaptive strategies tailored to your lifestyle. Remember, small changes in daily routines can significantly impact managing stress effectively. Incorporate regular breaks, set boundaries, and prioritize self-care in your schedule. Making a conscious effort to address stress can help shift your focus from negative patterns to healthier behaviours, ultimately leading to a more fulfilling life.

Using Positive Emotions to Reinforce Good Habits
Leveraging positive emotions can have a profound impact on habit formation. Accusing good feelings with specific behaviours creates a powerful incentive to repeat those behaviours in the future. This can take many forms, such as celebrating small victories, rewarding yourself after a workout, or simply reflecting on the joy that a particular habit brings to your life. Research demonstrates that when people experience positive emotions, they are more likely to engage in the habits that helped create those feelings in the first place. This connection makes establishing and maintaining routines easier because engaging in a good habit becomes a task to complete and a source of happiness and fulfilment. By intentionally focusing on the pleasure from your good habits, you can naturally reinforce them over time, making them an integral part of your lifestyle.Cultivating practices that evoke positive feelings in your daily routines can

significantly enhance your emotional well-being and strengthen your good habits. Start by integrating gratitude into your life; take a moment each day to think about what you appreciate, whether it's a sunny day, a good meal, or the support of a friend. This practice helps to shift your focus to the positive, creating a buffer against stress and negativity. Consider also incorporating mindfulness exercises that highlight the joy in routine activities. For example, while drinking your morning coffee, take a few moments to savour the taste and aroma, grounding yourself in the present moment. This mindfulness can turn everyday tasks into pleasurable experiences, enhancing your motivation to stick with them. Additionally, surround yourself with positivity, engage with uplifting content, connect with supportive people, and create an environment that encourages joy. All these elements combined can transform your daily activities into sources of happiness that bolster your commitment to positive habits.Ultimately, the magic happens when positive emotions become intertwined with your routine, making habits not just tasks but avenues for joy. Remember that the key is to find what resonates with you. Experiment with strategies to evoke positive feelings and see which ones feel most authentic and rewarding. Specifically, create small celebrations for your achievements and remember to acknowledge your progress, no matter how minor it may seem. When you cultivate a sense of enjoyment around your habits, you make them easier to maintain and enrich your life overall. Start today by identifying one habit you would like to strengthen and explore ways to make it a source of joy.

MAINTAINING HABITS OVER TIME

The Importance of Tracking Progress
Tracking your habits is essential for achieving long-term success. When you monitor your habits, you gain valuable insights into your behaviour and patterns, allowing you to make informed adjustments. Progress tracking creates accountability, which can be a powerful motivator. Seeing tangible changes, even small ones, reinforces your commitment and boosts your confidence. Furthermore, tracking helps you identify what works and what doesn't, which is crucial for maintaining momentum over time. Instead of relying on memory or vague feelings about progress, having concrete data allows you to celebrate minor victories and learn from setbacks without dwelling on them.Various tracking methods can be adopted to measure your habit performance effectively. One popular approach is to use a habit tracker app, which digitizes the process and often includes features like reminders and analytics. Alternatively, a simple bullet journal or planner can be a powerful tool for manual tracking. Writing things down reinforces commitment and lets you reflect on your journey. Another effective method is to establish a routine where you dedicate a few minutes to assess your progress at the end of each day, noting successes and areas for improvement. This reflection period strengthens your awareness and allows you to pivot when necessary.Make it a habit to review your progress regularly, weekly or monthly. This reflective practice will help you stay aligned with your long-term goals and ensure you're not

veering off course. Consider incorporating visual aids like charts or graphs to see your progress in real terms. They can serve as powerful motivators that keep the journey enjoyable. Ultimately, remember that consistency in tracking is key even when you may not feel like it; recording your efforts can reinforce responsibility and keep your end goal firmly in sight, making success more attainable.

Strategies for Long-Term Habit Maintenance
Learning techniques that promote the sustained practice of good habits is essential for long-term success. One effective method is to make your habits evident and appealing. This can be achieved by linking your new habits to specific environmental cues or daily routines. For example, if you want to develop a habit of drinking more water, place a glass by your bedside each night. When you wake up, the visual cue will remind you to hydrate.Additionally, incorporating the habit into a pre-existing routine can boost adherence. If you already have a morning routine, adding a few moments of stretching or deep breathing immediately after brushing your teeth can make the transition smoother. Another helpful technique is to keep your habits small and manageable. Focus on consistency over intensity; doing a little bit every day leads to more sustainable change than occasional bouts of high effort. Establishing a reward system where you celebrate small wins can also reinforce positive behaviour and encourage persistence.Understanding the role of periodic evaluation in habit maintenance is crucial for continued progress. Regularly assessing your habits lets you identify what's working and what might need adjustment. Consider setting aside time weekly or monthly to reflect on your habits. During these evaluations, ask yourself how you feel about the habits you are practising. Are they still aligned with your goals? Are there external factors that have made some habits more challenging? You can tailor your approach to fit your evolving needs by answering these questions. Moreover, tracking your progress through journals, apps, or a simple checklist can provide insight into your consistency

and motivate you to stay on course. Remember, habits are not set in stone; being flexible and open to change can lead to more effective habit maintenance and personal growth. One practical tip to enhance your habit maintenance strategy is to find an accountability partner. This could be a friend, family member, or colleague with similar goals or interests. Having someone to discuss your progress with creates a support system that encourages both of you to stay committed. You can set up regular check-ins, share successes, and discuss challenges. This collaborative approach makes the journey enjoyable and strengthens your resolve to stick to your habits for the long haul.

Dealing with Setbacks and Rebuilding Momentum

Recognizing common setbacks in habit maintenance is crucial for building lasting change. Life often presents challenges that can derail even the most dedicated individuals. From unexpected stressors to changes in routine, setbacks can take many forms, such as missing a workout, skipping a meditation session, or failing to stick to a healthy eating plan. A vital first step in addressing these challenges is acknowledging that setbacks are a normal part of the process. Understanding this can reduce guilt and frustration, making it easier to refocus on your goals. Once you recognize a setback, it's essential to identify the triggers. Were you feeling stressed? Did a busy schedule lead to skipping out on your habits? After placing the trigger, you can strategize on how to prevent similar situations in the future or develop a flexible plan that allows you to adapt without abandoning your goals. This might include creating reminders, seeking support from friends, or adjusting your routine when life becomes hectic. Formulating strategies for regaining momentum after a lapse is equally essential. The first step is to be kind to yourself. Rather than falling into a negative spiral of self-criticism, focus on what you can do moving forward. Allow yourself to regroup and assess the situation without judgment. A helpful technique is to set small, achievable goals that can serve as stepping stones back into your routine. For instance, start with a short walk or a few minutes of stretching instead of jumping back into an entire workout routine. This creates a sense of accomplishment and helps you regain your confidence. Another practical approach is establishing a support system that encourages you to share your struggles and victories. Engage with peers or a community that can provide motivation and accountability. Additionally, consider journaling your experience. Writing about the setbacks, how you felt, and the steps you took to overcome them can give you valuable insights into your patterns and reinforce your commitment to rebuilding momentum. Remember, progress is often not linear, and each small step forward is a step toward success. Implementing these practical steps can significantly enhance your ability to bounce back from setbacks. Think of maintaining habits as a dance; there will be missteps, but with awareness and techniques to regain balance, you can continue to sway to your rhythm. A good tip is to embrace flexibility in your approach. Life is dynamic, and adapting your methods while keeping your goals in sight will ensure you enjoy the journey rather than be disheartened by the occasional stumble.

HABIT CHANGE AND IDENTITY

Shifting Your Identity to Support New Habits
Identity plays a crucial role in habit formation, often serving as the foundation upon which our behaviours are built. When individuals see themselves in a particular way, their actions align with that self-perception. For instance, if a person defines themselves as 'an athlete,' they are more likely to engage in activities that reflect that identity, such as regular exercise and healthy eating. Conversely, if someone identifies as 'someone who doesn't exercise,' they may struggle to incorporate fitness into their life. This illustrates the powerful influence of identity on our choices and routines. Changing habits often feels challenging because it requires more than just altering actions; it necessitates a shift in self-concept. Understanding this relationship between identity and behaviour is essential for anyone looking to make lasting change.Redefining your self-image is vital to aligning your identity with the habits you want to cultivate. Start by consciously choosing statements that reflect the person you wish to become. Instead of saying, I want to be fit, try, I am a healthy person. Embracing this new self-image can be a powerful motivator, encouraging actions consistent with how you envision yourself. Visualization techniques can also be beneficial. Picture yourself engaging in your new habits and enjoying the benefits they bring. This mental rehearsal reinforces the identity you are building.Furthermore, surround yourself with people who embody the identity you aspire to. Their influence can help

solidify your transformation and provide support during your journey. Remember, the stronger your new self-image grows, the easier it becomes to adopt new behaviours that resonate with it. As you embark on this journey of identity transformation, consider keeping a journal to document your thoughts and progress. Write down the new identity you are adopting alongside the habits you wish to cultivate. Reflecting on your growth can enhance your commitment and clarify when challenges arise. Remember that shifting your identity is a gradual process, requiring patience and persistence. Focus on small, consistent changes and celebrate your successes along the way. This approach will reinforce your new self-image and make the journey enjoyable. By embracing a new identity, you are laying a solid foundation for sustainable habits that align with your aspirations and values.

The Role of Self-Perception in Behavior Change
Self-perception plays a crucial role in shaping our motivations and behaviours. When individuals see themselves as capable and worthy, they are more likely to take positive actions that align with their goals. Conversely, poor self-perception can lead to feelings of inadequacy, resulting in self-doubt and avoidance of challenges. Understanding this connection can empower individuals to harness their self-view to foster motivation. For example, when someone identifies as healthy, they naturally gravitate toward behaviours that reinforce that identity, such as exercising, eating nutritious food, and making mindful choices. This creates a positive feedback loop where enhanced self-perception fuels further motivation and desirable behaviours. On the other hand, negative self-perceptions can trap individuals in a cycle of failure, where the belief in their inability to change discourages attempts at growth or development.Enhancing positive self-perception can be approached through various effective methods. One practical strategy is the practice of self-affirmation. Regular self-affirmation exercises allow individuals to reflect on their strengths and achievements, fostering a more positive self-image. Additionally, surrounding oneself with

supportive and positive influences can significantly enhance self-perception. The language we use when we talk to ourselves matters profoundly. Transforming negative self-talk into constructive and encouraging inner dialogue can shift our perception. Another valuable approach involves setting small, achievable goals. Accomplishing these manageable tasks builds confidence and challenges negative beliefs, proving to oneself that progress is possible. Consistently celebrating even minor achievements reinforces a sense of competence and propels further action.Incorporating mindfulness practices can also contribute to a healthier self-perception. Individuals can separate their identity from their mistakes or weaknesses by cultivating awareness of thoughts and feelings without judgment, creating space for growth. Lastly, remember that self-perception is not static; it evolves. Engaging in new experiences and stretching beyond comfort zones can reveal previously unrecognized strengths and abilities. Individuals can create a foundation for sustainable behaviour change that aligns with their aspirations by consciously enhancing self-perception.

Aligning Habits with Personal Values

Aligning habits with core personal values is crucial for leading a fulfilling life. Your daily behaviours reflect what truly matters to you, creating a sense of authenticity and purpose. This alignment fosters a more profound commitment to your routines because it isn't just about achieving goals and living by your beliefs. For instance, if one of your core values is health, habits like exercising, eating well, and getting enough sleep take on a new meaning. They become not just actions to perform but expressions of who you are and what you stand for. The importance of this alignment lies in the motivation it generates. When your habits resonate with your values, pursuing them feels less like a chore and more like a natural extension of your identity. This intrinsic motivation leads to more sustainable habits and greater satisfaction.To evaluate your current habits against your values, start by clearly identifying your core values. Take the time to write them down, which can add clarity to what you indeed hold dear. Next, reflect on your daily habits and routines. Consider how each habit aligns or conflicts with your identified values. For example, disconnecting may drain your energy and sense of fulfilment if you value family time but often work late. By assessing this gap, you can uncover deeper motivations for change. The evaluation process can initially feel uncomfortable, especially if you're faced with habits that do not serve you. However, understanding the why behind your habits provides insight into how to make adjustments that bring your actions more in line with your values. As you reflect and evaluate, ask yourself, " Does this habit connect me to my values? How does this behaviour align with the person I want to be?It's essential to remember that progress is not always linear. Realigning habits with your values takes time and persistence. Start small by integrating one or two value-aligned habits into your daily routine. For example, if one of your values is creativity, you might set aside ten minutes daily to write or engage in a creative hobby. Gradually, as you build these habits, you'll find that they enhance your daily experiences and reinforce your values, leading to a more authentic and satisfying life. A practical tip: consider journaling your experiences with these new habits, noting how they make you feel about your values. This practice can deepen your understanding of your motivations and keep you accountable as you navigate your path toward alignment.

THE INFLUENCE OF TECHNOLOGY ON HABITS

Digital Tools for Habit Tracking
Modern technology has introduced a plethora of digital tools that enhance the practice of habit tracking, catering to various preferences and lifestyles. Habit-tracking applications are now available across multiple platforms, allowing users to quantify their progress and stay motivated. Tools like Habitica gamify the habit-forming process, turning daily tasks into quests and making the journey more engaging. Other applications like Streaks or Loop Habit Tracker focus on simplicity, enabling users to record daily habits easily. Additionally, many applications offer customization options, allowing individuals to set specific goals, receive reminders, and analyze patterns through insightful graphs and statistics. This visualization can bolster motivation by showcasing progress and trends over time, making staying committed to established goals easier. By integrating reminders and notifications, these tools serve as constant nudges, helping users stay accountable and consistent in their habit-building efforts.However, while the advantages of using technology for habit formation are considerable, there are also drawbacks. The ease of access to numerous applications can lead to overwhelm, making it challenging for individuals to choose the best tool for their needs. Additionally, reliance on digital reminders can create a dependency, where users may find it difficult to adhere to habits

without technological support. Privacy concerns are also significant; many habit-tracking apps collect user data, which raises potential issues regarding personal information security. Moreover, technology may distract from the core purpose of habit tracking, shifting focus to the digital interface rather than the actual habit itself. The balance between leveraging technological innovations and maintaining intrinsic motivation must be carefully navigated to achieve sustainable habit formation effectively.To maximize the effectiveness of digital tools in habit tracking, it is essential to approach these resources mindfully. Instead of relying solely on technology, consider combining digital tools with traditional methods, like journaling or writing goals down on paper. This dual approach can enhance awareness and personal commitment. Additionally, set specific parameters for how often and in what ways you will use these tools to reduce the risk of distraction. Limit notifications to essential updates and celebrate small victories along the way, as these celebrations can bolster motivation. By taking control of your habit-tracking process and integrating digital tools in a balanced way, you can foster the change you aspire to achieve.

The Role of Apps in Behavior Change
Smartphone apps have emerged as powerful tools for facilitating positive behaviour change across various aspects of life. They provide an accessible and engaging way for individuals to track habits, monitor progress, and receive real-time feedback. By leveraging technology, these apps can offer personalized experiences that cater to users' specific needs and lifestyles. The convenience of mobile access ensures that users can engage with the app anytime, anywhere, reducing barriers often associated with traditional behaviour modification methods. Moreover, many apps use gamification techniques to motivate users, turning the usually daunting task of changing habits into a more enjoyable and rewarding experience. This makes it easier for individuals to stay committed to their goals, as continuous interaction and supportive prompts keep them on track.Effective

habit-forming apps share several key features that enhance their ability to support behaviour change. First, precise goal-setting capabilities allow users to define their goals, ensuring their objectives are specific and attainable. Feedback mechanisms are also crucial; apps that provide timely updates on users' performance create a sense of accountability, helping to reinforce positive actions. Additionally, reminders and notifications serve as gentle nudges, triggering users to engage with their new habits regularly. Social sharing features can further amplify encouragement, enabling users to connect with friends or a community for support and motivation. Lastly, a user-friendly design contributes to an enjoyable experience; when navigating the app is seamless, users are more likely to stick with it and develop sustainable habits.Find one that resonates with your personal goals and preferences to maximize your success with behaviour change apps. Take the time to explore different options until you find one that feels intuitive and supportive. Set clear guidelines for yourself in the app, and don't hesitate to adjust your expectations as your journey progresses. Enlisting the help of friends can also make a difference; share your goals and progress with someone who can cheer you on. This accountability is often a significant motivating factor. By understanding how apps function and what features work best for you, you can harness the power of technology in your journey towards lasting behaviour change.

Navigating Distractions in a Digital Age
Digital distractions have seeped into every corner of our lives, altering our habits in ways we might not initially notice. Notifications from social media, constant emails, and endless content streams can distract our attention from what truly matters. This incessant barrage of information creates a fragmented attention span that diminishes our ability to focus intensely on tasks. Studies show that it can take numerous minutes to regain our focus entirely when we are interrupted. Over time, these disruptions can affect our productivity,

creativity, and even our mental health, leading to increased stress and anxiety. Recognizing the impact of these distractions is the first step in reclaiming your time and attention.Creating a space that encourages focus is essential to minimise distractions in your environment. Begin by identifying the sources of your digital noise. Is it your phone buzzing every few minutes? Is your workspace littered with unused devices? Removing or silencing these potential distractions can cultivate a more-centred work environment. Consider setting specific times to check emails or social media rather than allowing these activities to interrupt your flow at random intervals. Implementing screen time limits or utilizing apps that block distracting websites during work hours can also help. By intentionally setting boundaries around your digital consumption, you can carve out a space where focus can thrive.Ultimately, it's about finding the balance that works for you. Small changes can lead to significant improvements in your ability to concentrate. For instance, dedicating the first hour of your day to deep work, free from distractions, can create a productive rhythm that carries through the rest of your tasks. Think about establishing a 'distraction-free zone' in your home or workspace, complete with everything you need to focus on. You can control your time and enhance your overall productivity by consciously choosing when and how to engage with your digital devices.

SOCIAL SUPPORT AND HABIT FORMATION

The Importance of Accountability Partners

Accountability partners play a crucial role in enhancing commitment to new habits. When individuals embark on the journey to adopt a new behaviour, whether exercising regularly, eating healthier, or improving productivity, going solo can lead to wavering motivation. Having an accountability partner creates an external commitment that reinforces one's resolve. It's the knowledge that someone else is invested in your success. This connection fosters a sense of responsibility, encouraging you to show up and do the work. When the motivation wanes— and it inevitably does— an accountability partner can remind you of your goals, help you navigate obstacles, and celebrate your progress. This shared experience can also create a social dynamic that cultivates encouragement, support, and accountability, making it easier to stick to plans even when the enthusiasm fades.Finding and maintaining relationships with accountability partners involves intentional steps. Start by seeking out individuals who share similar goals or challenges. This could be a friend, family member, coworker, or even someone from an online community dedicated to self-improvement. Once you've identified potential partners, it's essential to establish clear expectations. Discuss how often you want to check in with each other, whether it's weekly calls, daily texts, or a shared online platform. Regular communication reinforces the commitment to your goals. Be open and honest about your struggles and successes; vulnerability fosters deeper connections and understanding. Moreover, as you establish this partnership, consider setting up structured ways to keep each other accountable, such as tracking progress, sharing insights, and brainstorming solutions to challenges that arise. Building and sustaining this relationship can evolve as you grow, so remain adaptable and receptive to change as you pursue your goals together.Utilizing accountability partners can significantly increase the likelihood of achieving your desired habits and goals. Effective partnerships thrive on trust, respect, and shared aspirations. When you commit to regular check-ins and supportive dialogues, you foster a productive environment for both you and your partner. A practical tip to enhance this relationship is to schedule "accountability dates" where you can reflect on progress and adjust your strategies together. This strengthens your bond and clarifies your intentions, ensuring that both partners are aligned and motivated.

Building a Supportive Community
Community support plays a vital role in building and maintaining habits. It provides a sense of belonging and accountability that encourages individuals to stay on track with their goals. When people surround themselves with others who share similar commitments, they experience increased motivation and a shared understanding of the challenges of habit formation. Being part of a community creates opportunities for individuals to celebrate small victories, share insights, and offer support during setbacks. This shared experience can significantly reduce feelings of isolation and boost persistence in the habit-building journey.Discovering avenues for creating or joining supportive, habit-focused communities can significantly enhance your ability to form lasting habits. Many options exist, from local group meetings in person to online forums where individuals

can connect globally. Consider joining specialized classes or workshops focusing on specific habits, such as fitness groups or writing clubs. Social media platforms can also be powerful tools for connecting with others who share your interests; look for hashtags or groups aligned with your goals. Establishing regular touchpoints with these communities through meet-ups or virtual discussions can foster deeper connections and provide the encouragement needed to thrive.Creating rituals within your community can further enhance the support system. For instance, setting up regular check-ins or challenge events can cultivate a sense of camaraderie and mutual commitment. Whether you engage in shared activities or meet to discuss progress and hurdles, maintaining these connections will strengthen your resolve and ensure you have a support network on this journey.

Sharing Progress to Strengthen Commitment
Sharing your goals and progress can significantly enhance your motivation. When you articulate your aspirations aloud or write them down for others to see, you create an external commitment that complements your internal drive. This process encourages accountability, making you more likely to take the necessary steps to achieve those goals. Furthermore, sharing your milestones, whether big or small, fosters a sense of accomplishment that boosts your confidence and energizes your efforts. For example, discussing your fitness journey with friends or family keeps you committed to your routine and supports your network. Social interactions surrounding your objectives can ignite a shared enthusiasm that propels you forward, transforming solitary efforts into a collective pursuit of success.Effectively communicating your achievements is essential for the motivation above to take root. There are various methods to share your progress that can resonate with those around you. A straightforward approach is to utilize social media platforms where you can document your journey, interact with like-minded individuals, and receive positive reinforcement

through comments and likes. Another method involves regular check-ins with a mentor, coach, or accountability partner; these conversations can reinforce your dedication while highlighting your progress. Writing a blog or even keeping a personal journal that you're willing to share can be beneficial. In this way, you encapsulate not only what you accomplished but also what challenges you faced and how you overcame them. This narrative empowers you by creating a storyline around your achievements, making them more meaningful for you and those who read about them.Ultimately, sharing your progress is about embracing vulnerability and authenticity. When you openly communicate your journey, you reinforce your commitment and inspire others to share their journeys. Consider setting specific moments for reflection and sharing, weekly or monthly, to keep the motivation flowing. By turning your achievements into a collective experience, the motivation that arises can lead to continuous improvement and persistence in achieving goals. Remember, sharing is not merely a celebration; it's a strategic approach to sustaining your ambition.

ADVANCED TECHNIQUES FOR HABIT CHANGE

Visualization and Habit Success
Visualization can significantly enhance the likelihood of successful habit change by activating the brain's simulation mechanisms. When you vividly imagine yourself performing the desired habit, your mind often cannot distinguish between actual practice and mental rehearsal. This cognitive practice makes it easier to adopt the behaviour in real life. For instance, if you visualize yourself confidently exercising regularly, you create a mental map of that routine, making it feel more familiar and achievable. The more detailed your visualization, the more effective it can be; think about what you are wearing, how you feel, and even the surrounding environment. This exercise primes your brain for success, increasing your motivation and readiness to act. Visualization bridges the mental and the physical, turning desires into tangible plans and paving the way for genuine progress.Practical visualization techniques are essential for anyone looking to build lasting habits. One effective method involves creating a 'visualization board' to collage images, words, and quotes representing your goals and desired habits. This board is a daily reminder of your objectives, reinforcing your commitment each time you see it. Another technique is to set aside time each day for a short visualization session. During this time, find a quiet space, close your eyes, and vividly imagine

yourself engaging in your new habit. Use all your senses—what do you see, hear, and feel? Making these sessions a routine part of your day can establish a powerful mental anchor that strengthens your resolve to adopt the new behaviour.One simple but powerful tip for effectively applying visualization is combining it with affirmation statements. When you visualize yourself succeeding in your new habit, speak affirmations out loud or silently that reinforce your belief in your ability to succeed. Phrases like "I am becoming an expert at maintaining my daily exercise" or "I easily stick to my new routine" can enhance your visualization experience. By pairing visual images with positive affirmations, you create a synergistic effect that boosts motivation and sharpens your focus on achieving your goals. This technique can be beneficial during challenging moments when your resolve may waver.

The Role of Meditation in Habit Formation
Meditation can play a crucial role in supporting mindfulness and facilitating habit change. By cultivating awareness, meditation enables individuals to observe their thoughts and behaviours without judgment. This heightened awareness is essential for identifying and understanding the habits that shape daily life. When you meditate, you create a mental space that allows you to see habitual patterns. You can recognize triggers and responses associated with your habits, which is the first step toward meaningful change. For example, someone trying to quit smoking might use meditation to become mindful of the cravings they experience, recognizing them as temporary feelings rather than insurmountable urges. This understanding empowers individuals to break free from automatic responses and fosters the ability to make conscious choices instead.Integrating mindfulness techniques into daily routines can significantly enhance the habit-formation process. Simple mindfulness practices like focused breathing or mindful walking can seamlessly be woven into everyday activities. For instance, while brushing your teeth, you might focus intently on the toothbrush's sensations and the

toothpaste's taste. This reinforces the habit of oral hygiene and enhances your mindfulness skills. Another technique involves setting reminders to practice mindfulness throughout the day; a small alarm can prompt you to take a few deep breaths or take a quick body scan. By incorporating these techniques into regular activities, mindfulness becomes a part of your routine, making it easier to cultivate new habits. The key is to start small and build on these moments, gradually deepening your practice and reinforcing the association between mindfulness and positive behaviour changes.One helpful piece of information for anyone looking to use meditation for habit formation is to track your progress. Keeping a journal can be an effective way to observe how mindfulness impacts your habits over time. Write about your meditation experiences and reflect on any changes you notice in your behaviours or attitudes. This practice fosters greater self-awareness and reinforces your commitment to habit change. Tracking your progress will help you stay motivated and identify what works best for you, leading to more sustainable habits.

Experimenting with Habit Interventions
Trial and error serves as a powerful approach to discovering effective habits. This method highlights the importance of experimentation in understanding what truly works for us as individuals. Every person has unique circumstances that make certain habits more or less effective. By engaging in trial and error, you allow yourself to explore different methods and strategies without fearing failure. Instead of seeing setbacks as obstacles, consider them valuable learning opportunities. Through this process, one can fine-tune their approach to build habits that align with their values and lifestyle. Recognizing that not every method will resonate with you paves the way for tailored solutions that can lead to real, lasting change.Designing and implementing personal habit experiments requires a thoughtful yet flexible approach. Start by identifying a specific habit you wish to develop or change. Measurably frame this habit; for instance, if you want to exercise more, specify the duration

and frequency. Next, various strategies should be considered to adopt this habit. These include setting reminders, finding an accountability partner, or selecting a specific time of day for practice. Creating a simple timeline for experimentation can be incredibly useful. Try each method for a set period, adjusting based on what feels correct and effective. Reflect regularly on your progress and feelings, documenting what works and what doesn't. This documentation will help you identify patterns and refine your future experiments.One practical tip for successful habit experimentation is to embrace flexibility. While having a plan is essential, being open to changing your approach based on your evolving needs and experiences is equally important. If a method is not resonating, don't hesitate to pivot and try something else. The beauty of experimentation lies in its capacity to reveal insights about your preferences and inclinations. Staying curious about your habits will enhance your understanding of yourself and galvanize your commitment to personal growth. Continuous reflection can create profound insights and more pronounced changes, leading to a sustainable and fulfilling habit-building journey.

REFLECTION AND CONTINUOUS IMPROVEMENT

The Cycle of Habit Reflection
Regular reflection on habits is crucial for personal growth and self-awareness. It allows individuals to evaluate their behaviours, understand triggers, and recognize patterns that may be beneficial or detrimental. When you allocate time to reflect, you become more in tune with your actions and gain insights into how these habits shape your thoughts and feelings. This deeper understanding can lead to better decision-making and goal-setting. Reflection creates a consistent cycle where you can assess what is working in your life and what needs adjustment, improving the natural outcome of the process.To effectively guide your habit reflection, it is essential to ask the right questions. Consider what habits are currently eating up your time or energy. Reflect on how these habits affect your productivity and emotional state. Ask yourself how you feel after engaging in a particular habit—does it energize or drain you? It's also beneficial to examine the circumstances surrounding a habit. What triggered it? Were there specific emotions or situations that led you to engage in it? These questions can help create a clear picture of your habits, facilitating a shift towards more empowering behaviours.Recognizing the cyclical nature of habit reflection can further enhance your growth. After identifying and analyzing your habits, take actionable steps to implement

change. Set specific, measurable goals that align with your desired outcomes. Document your progress and schedule regular intervals for reflection to reassess your habits. This ongoing process of noticing, questioning, and adjusting will create a sustainable path for personal development. Set aside a few minutes each day or week to engage in this practice; the insights gained can significantly influence your journey towards a fulfilled life.

Setting New Goals After Achieving Old Ones
After reaching a significant goal, it's essential to take a moment to reflect on your journey. This pause allows you to internalize your achievements and clarifies the next steps. Setting new, meaningful goals entails understanding your values and what excites you. Consider what you've learned from your past experiences and how those lessons can shape your future aspirations. Think about your cultivated habits and how they can serve as a foundation for new challenges. When establishing new goals, ensure they align with your passions and purpose. Instead of defaulting to societal expectations, focus on what resonates with your true self. This way, the journey becomes rewarding rather than merely a checklist of accomplishments.Assessing your progress is a vital part of fostering continuous growth and improvement. Regularly evaluating how far you've come can provide motivation and insights on areas needing adjustment. Reflect on your achievements, no matter how small, and recognize the effort that went into reaching them. Self-assessment can be done through journaling or informal discussions with trusted friends or mentors. Ask yourself what strategies worked well, what challenges arose, and how you navigated them. This reflective practice cultivates resilience and adaptability, setting a positive tone for future endeavours. Embrace constructive feedback and allow yourself the space to learn from setbacks, as they often provide the most significant lessons.Engaging in goal-setting is not a one-time event but rather an ongoing process. As you achieve your goals, new opportunities will likely

emerge, demanding you adapt and reevaluate your trajectory. Embrace this fluidity and stay open to change. Keeping a growth mindset allows you to see setbacks as stepping stones rather than obstacles. A practical tip for maintaining momentum is to establish a routine check-in practice. This could be monthly reflections where you assess your current goals, adjust your strategies, and set new targets based on evolving interests and circumstances. This consistent practice will align you with your aspirations and build the resilience and adaptability necessary for long-term success.

Embracing a Growth Mindset in Habit Formation
Recognizing the value of a growth mindset is crucial in supporting habit change. People with a growth mindset believe their abilities and intelligence can be developed through dedication and hard work. This perspective creates a love for learning and resilience essential for overcoming challenges during habit formation. When attempting to create new habits or break old ones, having this mindset allows individuals to view setbacks not as failures but as opportunities for growth. For instance, if someone aims to exercise regularly but misses a few sessions, they can analyze what went wrong instead of feeling defeated and adjust their approach. This approach fosters a healthier relationship with the process of change but also encourages consistent effort regardless of the outcome.Exploring strategies to cultivate and reinforce a growth mindset can significantly enhance habit formation. One effective strategy is to practice self-reflection regularly. Taking time to assess personal thoughts and reactions can help identify fixed mindsets, such as feelings of inadequacy or frustration. Replacing these thoughts with affirmations of progress and potential can reinforce a growth-oriented perspective. Additionally, surrounding oneself with supportive individuals with a growth mindset can be beneficial; discussing challenges and strategies with others fosters an environment where learning and resilience are celebrated. Engaging in ongoing education through reading,

workshops, or personal projects feeds the growth mindset. The more knowledge and skills one acquires, the more confidence one gains in one's capacity to change and develop new habits.Implementing a growth mindset in habit formation means understanding that change is a journey. Every small step toward a new habit is a move toward transformation. Remember that persistence is key; even the most successful individuals face numerous obstacles before achieving their goals. Keep pushing forward, celebrate minor victories along the way, and remember that with the right mindset, every effort enhances your ability to adapt and flourish.

THE ROLE OF PSYCHOLOGY IN HABITS

Cognitive Behavioral Theory and Habits

Cognitive behavioural principles play a significant role in understanding habits' formation and maintenance. This theory's core is the idea that our thoughts, feelings, and behaviours are interconnected. Regarding habits, recognizing how our thoughts influence our actions can lead to healthier behavioural patterns. By identifying negative thought patterns that trigger undesirable habits, we can begin to alter those thoughts to foster positive changes. For example, if someone feels overwhelmed by exercising, they might avoid it altogether. However, by challenging that thought—perhaps by reminding themselves of the benefits of exercise or starting with small, manageable goals—they can gradually build a more positive association with the activity. This interplay between cognition and behaviour is central to habit formation and transformation.Fostering a supportive environment is another critical factor in habit formation. Surrounding oneself with positive influences and resources can reinforce good habits. For example, joining a support group or finding a workout partner can provide motivation and accountability. Finally, integrating mindfulness practices can enhance self-awareness, leading to better control over impulses and automatic responses. This awareness helps individuals pause and reflect before acting, allowing them to make better choices aligned with their desired habits. A practical tip for anyone looking to change or develop a habit is to start small and stay consistent. Making gradual changes rather than overwhelming oneself with drastic shifts can lead to lasting improvements.

Motivation and Its Impact on Habits

Different types of motivation can significantly influence the success of habit formation. Intrinsic motivation, which comes from within, often leads to more sustainable habits. Individuals who engage in activities because they find them enjoyable or fulfilling are more likely to stick with them over time. For instance, someone who exercises because they genuinely enjoy the activity is likelier to maintain that routine than someone who only exercises to lose weight. On the other hand, extrinsic motivation, driven by external rewards or pressures, can be effective in the short term but may wane once the external incentives are removed. It's crucial to recognize that the type of motivation can dictate how easily and effectively one can form and maintain new habits. Understanding these dynamics allows individuals to make informed choices about approaching habit formation.Enhancing motivation for sustained habit change involves combining strategies that focus on intrinsic and extrinsic factors. Setting specific, achievable goals can foster inherent motivation by providing a clear path and a sense of accomplishment. Visual reminders, such as habit trackers or inspirational posters, can boost motivation by keeping the desired behaviour front and centre in daily life. Furthermore, creating a supportive environment that encourages habit change, such as surrounding oneself with like-minded individuals, can provide the necessary encouragement and reinforcement. Engaging in self-reflection to identify personal values and align them with new habits can deepen intrinsic motivation, making the change feel more meaningful. Finding ways to make the new habit enjoyable or incorporating rewards for achieving milestones can enhance motivation further.It's beneficial to start small and build gradually to solidify your habits. This approach helps create a sense of accomplishment, further reinforcing motivation. Consider integrating habits into your existing routines, making them feel less like an obligation and more like a natural part of your day. Celebrate your wins, no matter how small. This positive reinforcement can strengthen your motivation and promote a cycle of success. Remember, the journey of habit formation is personal; understanding your unique drivers of motivation will help pave the way for lasting change.

The Habit Loop: Cue, Routine, Reward
The habit loop consists of three essential components: cue, routine, and reward. Understanding these mechanics is crucial for uncovering how habits are formed and maintained. The cue is a trigger that starts the habit. It can be anything from a specific time of day to an emotional state or even a location. For example, walking into your kitchen might signal a cue to grab a snack. This cue leads to the routine, the behaviour you exhibit in response to the trigger. In this case, the routine would be reaching for a bag of chips. Finally, the reward reinforces the habit; it's what you gain from completing the routine. This could be the satisfaction from eating something tasty, providing a sense of pleasure or relief. Over time, the habit loop becomes automatic, with cues and rewards reinforcing the routine, often without conscious thought.Manipulating your habit loop can be a powerful strategy for improvement. To do this effectively, start by identifying your current cues and routines. Keeping a journal can help track what prompts your habitual behaviours and what rewards you seek. Once you determine your cues, consider how you can change your routines while maintaining similar rewards. For instance, if your cue is stress leading to a habit of snacking on unhealthy foods, you might change your routine to take a brisk walk instead while still seeking a reward of stress relief.Attaching a new reward to a positive behaviour can enhance its appeal. For example, you might reward yourself with a favourite show or a small treat after completing a workout. By actively reshaping your habit loop,

you're not just eliminating unwanted habits but also building new, healthier ones that can lead to long-term change. As you embark on this journey of habit manipulation, remember that consistency is key. Minor adjustments to your cues and routines, reinforced with compelling rewards, can create significant shifts in behaviour over time. Finding accountability, whether through friends, family, or an app, can also provide motivation. Remember that habits don't change overnight; patience and perseverance are essential. Utilize these insights and strategies to craft habits that serve you better, allowing you to lead a more intentional and fulfilling life.

THE POWER OF THINKING PATTERNS

How Thoughts Shape Behavior

The way we think profoundly influences how we act. Every time you encounter a situation, your mind processes it through various thought patterns that can shape your behavioural responses. Negative thinking, such as self-doubt or pessimism, often leads to avoidance behaviours or adverse outcomes, while positive thinking fosters resilience and proactive actions. Research in psychology shows that the connection between thoughts and behaviours is intricate; recognizing your thinking patterns is the first step to changing your behaviour. By becoming aware of your automatic thoughts, especially those that arise in challenging situations, you can see how they directly impact your actions. For instance, if you often think, "I will fail," you might freeze in a performance situation or avoid it altogether, confirming your beliefs. On the other hand, shifting to a more empowering thought like, "I have prepared well and can do this," can shift your behaviour from avoidance to proactive engagement.Developing a habit of cultivating constructive thoughts is essential for promoting positive habits. One effective strategy is to practice positive affirmations. These simple yet powerful statements you repeat to yourself are designed to challenge and eliminate self-sabotaging thoughts. Pairing affirmations with visualization techniques can further enhance their effectiveness. Imagine successfully handling a situation while reciting your affirmations. This mental rehearsal ingrains positive beliefs in your subconscious, making it easier to act on them in reality.Additionally, mindfulness can play a crucial role in managing your thoughts. You can create space between your thoughts and actions by being present and observing your thoughts without judgment. This awareness allows you to catch negative thoughts before they dictate your behaviour, giving you the control to redirect your responses positively. Start to nurture your thoughts each day, and watch how your behaviours evolve over time.Incorporating small practices into your daily routine can yield significant changes. Consider journaling your thoughts and emotions regularly. This helps illuminate recurring negative patterns, enabling you to challenge and reshape them. Create a 'thought challenge' where you identify and replace a negative thought with a positive counterpart. The more you engage in this process, the more natural it will become to gravitate toward thoughts that fuel productive behaviours. Change takes time, but consistently nurturing positive thinking creates a ripple effect, transforming your actions and life.

The Connection Between Beliefs and Habits
Personal beliefs play a crucial role in shaping our habits. Daily, our beliefs act as filters through which we interpret our experiences, guiding our responses and choices. When you believe in your ability to change, you create a positive feedback loop that encourages the development of healthy habits. For example, someone who thinks exercising regularly is essential for their well-being is more likely to integrate fitness into their daily routine. This belief fuels motivation, making it easier to stick to a regimen even on tough days. Conversely, if you believe that exercise is a chore or that you don't have the time, your choices will reflect that mindset, resulting in skipped workouts and missed growth opportunities. The beliefs we hold often dictate how we respond to obstacles and challenges. An optimistic person may bounce back from setbacks more readily than someone who sees challenges as insurmountable. This underlines the importance of examining and reshaping the beliefs we

unconsciously carry, as doing so can profoundly influence our ability to forge and maintain positive habits. To nurture habits effectively, it's essential to identify specific beliefs that hinder or support your progress. Certain self-limiting beliefs, such as thinking I'll never be good at this or I don't have what it takes, can create barriers to forming new habits. These negative beliefs can lead to avoidance behaviours, where you shy away from activities that could otherwise promote growth. Understanding these potentially harmful beliefs is the first step toward overcoming them. Conversely, beliefs reinforcing capability and development, like I can improve with practice or Every small step counts, encourage the necessity to adopt and maintain new habits. Cultivating a mindset centred around possibility rather than limitation empowers you to take actionable steps toward your goals. It's also valuable to periodically evaluate these beliefs to ensure they align with your current situation. As beliefs affect habits, changing your beliefs can significantly improve habit development. Recognizing the connection between your beliefs and behaviour offers a powerful insight that can lead to transformative change. To foster positive habit development, start by journaling about your beliefs. Write down your beliefs about your capabilities, goals, and potential barriers. Then, challenge any negative beliefs with evidence from your past successes or the experiences of others. Gradually replacing harmful beliefs with constructive ones can help reinforce a more supportive mindset, paving the way for habits that align with your true aspirations.

Cognitive Distortions Affecting Habit Formation

Several cognitive distortions can significantly hinder the process of habit formation. One common distortion is all-or-nothing thinking. This perspective leads individuals to view their efforts as binary; if they don't accomplish a goal perfectly, they perceive their attempts as failures. For instance, if a person aims to exercise five days a week but only manages three, they may abandon their routine altogether, believing they've messed up the whole week. Another prevalent distortion is overgeneralization, where individuals take one negative experience and extrapolate it to all future efforts. After missing a few days of a new habit, a person may conclude that they will never succeed at establishing that habit. Similarly, catastrophizing is a distortion where individuals imagine the worst possible scenarios from minor setbacks. If someone skips one workout, they might think they have lost their progress, leading to discouragement and giving up. The inner critic can further amplify these distortions, with negative self-talk reinforcing these false beliefs. When people believe they cannot change, their motivation to develop beneficial habits diminishes.Challenging these cognitive distortions is essential for successful habit formation. One effective strategy is cognitive restructuring, which involves identifying and replacing negative thoughts with more balanced, realistic ones. Instead of viewing a missed workout as a total failure, try reframing it as simply a part of the journey, recognizing that no one is perfect and that setbacks are normal. Practising self-compassion can also be transformative; treat yourself with the kindness and understanding you would offer a friend in a similar situation. Additionally, employing a technique called 'thought stopping' can interrupt unhelpful thought patterns. When a negative thought arises, remember to stop and reflect on its validity. Consider using a journal to document your thoughts, which allows you to analyze and challenge them more effectively. Setting realistic, incremental goals instead of aiming for perfection can foster a sense of accomplishment, making you more likely to stick with new habits over time. Establishing a routine can also anchor your new habits and provide stability amid the chaos of daily life.Practical techniques for tackling cognitive distortions can lead to meaningful progress in habit formation. Consider implementing small, achievable tasks instead of overwhelming goals. Celebrate minor successes, no matter how small, and view them as steps toward larger objectives. This creates a positive feedback loop that discourages negative thinking and promotes perseverance. Mindfulness or meditation can also enhance self-awareness, allowing you to recognize when cognitive distortions arise. By observing your thoughts without judgment, it's easier to create space for more constructive perspectives. Lastly, seeking support from others can provide additional motivation and encouragement, reminding you that you're not alone in this journey. Remember, progress is progress, no matter how small it may seem.

IDENTIFYING YOUR HABITS

Self-Assessment Techniques

Identifying your habits requires a keen awareness of your daily routines and behaviours. One effective self-assessment technique involves keeping a journal. You can uncover patterns and tendencies that might go unnoticed by jotting down your daily activities and feelings. Reflecting on these entries weekly allows you to see your habits in context, giving insight into which ones contribute positively to your life and may hinder your progress. Another helpful method is the habit tracker, a visual representation of your habits that can show you the frequency and consistency of certain behaviours. Various apps and printable templates are available, and just the act of tracking can motivate you to maintain positive habits while decreasing undesirable ones. Additionally, consider conducting self-reflection sessions where you quiz yourself about your choices and behaviours in specific situations, offering you deeper insights into your motivations and responses.Evaluating the effectiveness of your current habits involves honesty and critical thinking. It's essential to consider how each habit affects your emotional and physical well-being. Ask yourself questions like: Does this habit bring me joy? Does it help me achieve my goals? You could also try a scale method where you rate your habits from one to ten regarding their contribution to your life satisfaction. This straightforward assessment can highlight which habits are worth maintaining and which need rethinking or replacement. Additionally, gather feedback from trusted friends or coaches who might see patterns in your behaviour that you haven't noticed. This outside perspective can be incredibly valuable, revealing blind spots in your self-assessment.As you assess your habits, remember that change is an ongoing process. Regularly revisiting your self-assessments and being open to adapting your strategies will yield the best results. A practical tip is to set specific times for self-assessment, such as at the end of each week or month. This allows for structured reflection without feeling overwhelmed. This periodic check-in lets you stay aligned with your goals and consistently evaluate your habits' impact on your life.

Journaling for Habit Awareness
Journaling has emerged as a powerful tool for those seeking to increase their awareness of habits. When you take the time to document your daily actions and feelings, you create a deeper understanding of your routines and behaviours. Writing helps to crystallize thoughts and brings unconscious patterns into conscious awareness. This heightened awareness allows you to identify positive and negative habits, facilitating informed choices about which behaviours to encourage or modify. As you write, you can reflect on the triggers that lead to certain habits, paving the way for more mindful decision-making in the future. Over time, journaling can lead to significant insights into your motivations, showing you how habits intertwine with your emotions and overall mental health.Implementing journaling practices designed explicitly for habit tracking can further enhance your self-awareness. Start by setting aside a few minutes daily to reflect on your activities. One effective method is to create a habit journal with dedicated sections for various aspects of your life, such as health, productivity, and self-care. Record the habits you want to track, how they make you feel, and any patterns you observe. For instance, if you're tracking your exercise routine, note the time of day you work out, your energy levels, motivation, and any external factors influencing your performance. This structured approach keeps you accountable and allows for

adjustments based on your reflections. Integrating these practices into your routine will enable you to transform a simple journal into a powerful catalyst for understanding and improving your habits.To maximize the benefits of your journaling practice, consider ending each entry with a short plan for the following day. This could involve setting specific goals related to your habits or addressing any challenges you face. Writing down your intentions solidifies your commitment and provides a roadmap to follow. Over time, this proactive approach, combined with consistent reflection, can lead to profound changes in your behaviour, helping you to replace unproductive habits with those that align more closely with your goals and values.

Analyzing Triggers for Existing Habits

Understanding the cues that trigger your habits is the first step in transforming those behaviours. Think of cues as signals that initiate specific actions, often without conscious thought. These signals can be anything from a particular time of day, a location, an emotional state, or even another behaviour you routinely engage in. A classic example is how an alarm might prompt you to get out of bed and start your morning routine or how entering a kitchen at night might trigger the urge to snack. By becoming mindful of your surroundings and following patterns, you can pinpoint what cues lead to your habits. Keeping a journal or using a habit-tracking app can assist you in mapping these triggers out clearly. Observe what happens before you engage in a habit and take note of the context. Identifying these cues will empower you to be more aware of when to intervene or when to redirect your actions.Once you have identified your triggers, the next step is to explore ways to modify them for better habit control. A helpful technique is cue restructuring, which involves changing the environment where habits occur or altering the associated cues. For instance, redesigning your stress-relief strategy can help if stress triggers impulsive eating. Instead of immediately reaching for snacks when you feel stressed, you could replace that trigger with a more constructive action, such as taking a five-minute walk or practising deep breathing.Consider using reminders or visual cues in your living space to reinforce your desired habits. For example, if you are trying to exercise more, placing your workout clothes where you can see them each morning can prompt you to get moving. By substituting your current triggers with healthier ones, you can create new pathways for action that align with your goals.Maintaining awareness of your triggers and actively modifying them requires practice and resilience. It's important to remember that habit change is often a gradual process rather than a sudden transformation. Being patient with yourself during this journey is essential. Another practical tip is to develop a personal "cue-card" system—a set of cards where you write down the cues for both desired and undesired habits. Keeping these cards accessible can remind you of your goals as you navigate various daily situations. By actively working on recognizing and reshaping your triggers, you pave the way for sustainable habit change and personal growth.

THE CYCLE OF CHANGE

Stages of Change Model

The Stages of Change Model, also known as the Transtheoretical Model, offers a comprehensive framework for understanding how individuals make significant behavioural changes. This model breaks down the change process into five key stages: pre-contemplation, contemplation, preparation, action, and maintenance. In the pre-contemplation stage, a person may not even recognize that a change is necessary. As they move into contemplation, they begin to acknowledge the need for change but may still feel ambivalent. The preparation stage involves making plans and setting goals, while the action stage is where the individual actively works to alter their behaviour. Finally, the maintenance stage is about sustaining the new behaviour over time and preventing relapse. Familiarizing yourself with these stages can empower you to approach behaviour transformation in a structured way, making navigating challenges and celebrating successes easier.Recognizing which stage you are currently in is crucial for effectively progressing through the change process. If you find yourself in the pre-contemplation phase, it may be beneficial to reflect on the reasons for change and gather information to spark motivation. As you shift into contemplation, consider writing down the pros and cons of changing versus staying the same, which can help clarify your feelings. If you are in the preparation stage, set specific, achievable goals and outline the steps needed to reach them. During the action phase, seek social support and stay committed to the changes you've planned. If you have reached the maintenance stage, continue to self-reflect and develop strategies to manage potential setbacks, reinforcing your commitment to sustaining the change. Identifying your current stage provides clarity and informs the next steps you need to take.As you navigate these stages, a practical tip is to keep a journal detailing your thoughts and feelings about the changes you're attempting. Regularly writing about your experiences can help you track your progress, recognize patterns, and make informed adjustments to your strategies as needed. This reflection supports your journey and helps maintain your motivation as you move through the Stages of Change.

From Pre-Contemplation to Maintenance
The journey through the stages of change is a transformative experience, often filled with hopes, challenges, and personal revelations. It starts with pre-contemplation, where individuals may not even recognize the need for change. They might feel like their current habits are OK or that they cannot change due to various barriers. During this stage, it's crucial to foster awareness through conversations, reading, or gentle nudges from friends or community resources that highlight the consequences of their habits without imposing guilt. The goal is to start planting the seeds of introspection, creating an opening for future consideration of change.As individuals progress to the contemplation stage, they begin to reflect on their habits and the potential benefits of changing. This stage may be marked by ambivalence, where the desire to change is weighed against fear or resistance. Techniques such as journaling can help articulate these conflicting feelings and create clarity. Self-assessment tools can guide individuals in identifying the pros and cons of changing versus staying the same, thus igniting a stronger motivation to commit to action.When individuals reach the preparation stage, they are ready to plan for change. This is where specific strategies come into play. Setting achievable goals, finding support systems, and creating action plans can empower individuals to take those

first essential steps. They might seek community groups or professional help, allowing themselves to lean on others. This stage involves taking small, concrete actions that reinforce the intention to change while preparing their environment to support these new behaviours. As individuals move into the action stage, implementing changes becomes the focus. Tracking progress is vital here. Keeping a journal or using apps to monitor behaviour can provide insight and accountability. Celebrating small wins is also essential, as well as building motivation and reinforcing new habits. Learning to cope with setbacks is crucial, so embracing flexibility and resilience can help maintain momentum even when faced with challenges. Finally, in the maintenance stage, the goal is to sustain the change for the long term. This is where individuals can reflect on their journey, solidifying the new habits as a part of their identity. Strategies such as continued engagement with supportive communities, ongoing self-reflection, and regular goal reassessment can help individuals navigate this stage. Remembering that maintenance isn't a finish line, but part of an ongoing process is pivotal. A practical tip is establishing a routine where you regularly check in on your goals and celebrate your achievements, keeping the motivation alive and the change ingrained in daily life.

Relapse and How to Overcome It
Understanding the common causes of relapse is crucial for anyone on a recovery journey. Factors such as stress, environmental triggers, or even certain emotional states can lead to a slide back into old patterns. Anticipating these potential pitfalls can be the key to maintaining progress. For instance, recognizing that a relevant situation might provoke feelings of vulnerability allows you to prepare. Keeping a journal can be very helpful. Documenting feelings and situational triggers gives insight into patterns over time. This awareness is a protective measure, almost like a weather forecast for your mental health, helping you brace yourself against impending storms. Recovering from a relapse involves taking actionable steps that foster resilience and growth.

First, it is essential to assess the situation objectively. Understand what led to the relapse without judgment; this is not about guilt but learning. Reaching out for support is also vital. Whether with friends, family, or a support group, engaging in conversation helps process experiences and reframe the narrative. Establishing a self-care routine can significantly uplift your spirits. Engaging in activities that promote well-being, such as regular exercise, mindfulness practices, or even creative outlets, can restore a sense of control. Remember to set small, attainable goals in your recovery journey that allow for gradual improvement and reinforce a sense of achievement. Adopting a mindset of flexibility may enhance your ability to cope with future challenges. Life is unpredictable, and expecting perfection sets you up for disappointment. Instead, embrace the idea that setbacks are part of the journey and can offer invaluable lessons for growth. Maintain an open line of communication with yourself and others. Regularly check in on your feelings and progress, and don't hesitate to seek help. Keeping a balanced perspective and being kind to yourself during tough times will nurture resilience. When faced with a difficult moment, remind yourself of your strengths and previous successes to find that motivation again and keep moving forward.

BUILDING NEW HABITS

Setting SMART Goals for Habits

Setting SMART goals is crucial for anyone looking to form and maintain effective habits. The acronym SMART stands for Specific, Measurable, Achievable, Relevant, and Time-bound. Each component is vital in ensuring that your goals are clear and reachable. When your goals are specific, you know exactly what you want to achieve. For example, instead of aiming to get fit, specify that I want to run a 5k in under 30 minutes. Measurable goals allow you to track your progress; this could mean quantifying your runs each week or recording your time. Achievability encourages you to set goals that challenge you but are still attainable, keeping frustration at bay. Ensuring your relevant goals ties them to your broader life aspirations, making them more meaningful and motivating. Lastly, setting a time-bound framework helps create a sense of urgency. Instead of saying, "I want to exercise more," you might say, "I will exercise three times a week for the next two months." This deadline gives you a clear marker for success and helps prompt consistent action.Tailoring your goals for effective habit formation involves understanding how these elements interact with your context. Start by reflecting on your current behaviours and identify which habits you want to cultivate. Once pinpointing a desired behaviour, apply the SMART criteria to create an engaging goal. Break down your overarching goal into smaller, manageable habits. For instance, if your objective is to read more books, you might set a goal to read 20 pages daily for six weeks. This strategy makes the process more digestible and gradually reshapes your routine, reinforcing the new habit without overwhelming you.

Consistent review and adjustment of your goals are vital as well. As you track your progress and find areas for difficulty or ease, don't hesitate to tweak your goals to fit your evolving lifestyle better. This adaptability increases your likelihood of success and ensures you remain motivated.As you establish your SMART goals, consider keeping a habit journal. Document your daily actions, thoughts, and feelings related to your goals. This practice enhances self-reflection and helps you recognize patterns you might want to change or reinforce. Remember, habit formation is a journey; small, consistent steps often lead to significant long-term changes. Focusing on the incremental improvements you experience can strengthen your determination and enthusiasm.

The Importance of Small Wins

Celebrating small wins is essential for boosting motivation and enhancing overall well-being. When individuals recognize and celebrate minor milestones, they create a positive reinforcement loop that propels them toward larger goals. This practice feeds into the psychological principle of incremental progress. Each small win serves as a stepping stone, showcasing the advancement and fostering a sense of achievement. The brain releases dopamine, a neurotransmitter linked to pleasure and reward, when achieving even the most miniature goals. This biochemical reaction not only uplifts our mood but also encourages the pursuit of future objectives. In practical terms, acknowledging these small victories, whether through journaling or sharing with friends, transforms the overwhelming nature of long-term goals into manageable segments that feel attainable.To maximize small wins, structuring your goals thoughtfully is crucial. This involves breaking larger goals down into smaller, actionable tasks that can be accomplished within a shorter timeframe. Instead of setting a goal to 'get fit,' one might put a target to go for a 20-minute walk three times a week. This specific, measurable approach allows for regular check-ins and provides frequent opportunities for celebration. By clearly defining what constitutes a win, you create a roadmap that guides your actions and makes the effort feel rewarding. When you achieve these smaller tasks, take a moment to acknowledge the success. Whether through a small treat, a note to yourself, or simply a moment of self-praise, this practice can reinforce your motivation to continue pushing towards the bigger picture. Additionally, maintaining flexibility in your goals adds to the effectiveness of this strategy. Adjusting tasks based on progress keeps the momentum going without leading to feelings of defeat.Creating a culture of small wins is not only beneficial for individual motivation but can also enhance teamwork and collaboration in group settings. Encouraging a team to celebrate small milestones cultivates an environment where effort is acknowledged, and successes are recognized, no matter how trivial they seem. This shared sense of accomplishment can lead to increased morale and productivity. To implement this within a team, consider establishing regular check-ins focusing on what members have achieved, no matter how small. This encourages a collective acknowledgement of progress and fosters a supportive atmosphere. Always remember that every journey is built on small victories; embracing them is the key to sustained motivation and success. Start today by pinpointing a small goal you can achieve this week, and plan a way to celebrate once you accomplish it. It's in these small victories that the foundation for more remarkable achievements lies.

Habit Stacking for Success
The habit-stacking technique involves strategically pairing new and existing habits, allowing seamless integration into daily routines. By identifying a habit you already perform consistently, you can effectively layer a new behaviour on top of it. This method leverages the power of cues and rewards, making forming new habits less daunting. For example, if you already brush your teeth every morning, you can stack a new habit, like reading a few pages of a book, immediately after. Every time you brush your teeth, this ensures you'll be reminded to read, making it easier to cultivate the new habit without relying on willpower alone. The process creates a natural flow in your

routine and helps build a chain of positive behaviours reinforcing one another. To create personalized habit stacks, it's essential to consider how different habits can complement and enhance each other. Start by listing down the habits you wish to develop and identify what you already do consistently. Look for habits that align with your goals or enhance your well-being. For instance, consider stacking a meditation practice with your morning coffee ritual if mindfulness is essential. This approach can transform a seemingly mundane task into a decisive moment of reflection and focus. A successful habit stack feels effortless and enjoyable, so ensuring that the new habit adds value rather than feeling like an added burden is critical. Regularly review and adjust your stacks to maintain relevance to your current life situation and goals. As you embark on your journey of habit stacking, remember to be patient and observant. Change takes time, and the key to successful integration lies in your flexibility. Track your progress and celebrate small victories along the way. If a particular stack isn't working, don't hesitate to modify it or try a different combination. Documentation can be invaluable; maintain a journal where you reflect on your habit-stacking journey, noting what works and what doesn't. This enhances accountability and provides insights that will further refine your approach, leading you closer to a life of sustained success.

THE INFLUENCE OF ENVIRONMENT ON HABITS

The Role of Physical Space in Habit Formation

Your physical environment plays a crucial role in shaping your habits, influencing your motivation and ability to follow through. If you're trying to develop a new habit, the space around you can set you up for success or contribute to your struggles. Consider where you work or relax; a messy desk might hinder your productivity, while a clean, organized space could invigorate your focus and creativity. When your environment is cluttered, it adds mental noise that can distract you from your goals. The key is to create a setting that aligns with your desired habits, making them easier to adopt and sustain. For instance, if you're working on establishing a reading habit, having a comfortable chair and a well-lit corner with your favourite books readily accessible can invite you to spend time engaging with literature rather than scrolling through social media. Understanding how these environmental cues trigger certain behaviours is fundamental to habit formation.Small, actionable steps toward optimizing your environment can yield significant results in your habit formation journey. One practical tip to implement is establishing a designated habit zone in your home—create spaces tailored explicitly for the habits you wish to cultivate. If you're trying to instil a gratitude practice, for instance, keep a journal and pen beside your bed so that it's the first thing you see each morning.

This serves as a reminder and makes it easy for you to engage in that habit without too much thought or effort. By consciously arranging your physical space with intent, you can transform where you live and work into an environment that actively supports the habits you want to develop, making progress more natural and rewarding.

Social Influences on Habit Behavior
Social circles and peer pressures significantly shape our habits, often in ways we might not consciously recognize. When we surround ourselves with others who prioritize certain behaviours, we are more likely to adopt those same behaviours. For instance, if you often spend time with friends who enjoy fitness and prioritize healthy eating, you are more inclined to embody those habits yourself. This phenomenon is partly due to the desire for acceptance; we naturally mimic the actions of those around us, striving to fit into our social groups. Additionally, peer pressure's subtle yet powerful influence can make us more likely to engage in behaviours we might not otherwise consider. This could include everything from experimenting with new hobbies to adopting lifestyle changes. Therefore, understanding the impact of our social environment is crucial for anyone looking to modify their habits.To cultivate positive influences, consider actively seeking out relationships that support your growth and goals. One effective method is to engage in communities that foster the behaviours you aspire to adopt. Joining clubs, attending workshops, or participating in group activities related to your interests can connect you with like-minded individuals who encourage you. It's essential to evaluate your current social circles, too. Recognizing the dynamics at play can help you make more conscious choices about who to spend time with. Surrounding yourself with supportive, motivated people can create an uplifting milieu where positive habits flourish while distancing yourself from those who engage in detrimental behaviours can strengthen your resolve.Peer influence is not just about avoiding negativity but also about promoting positivity. Forming positive habits

can be enhanced through accountability. Share your goals with those who uplift you, and consider finding an accountability partner with similar aspirations. This can create a sense of mutual support and motivation. It's never too late to reshape your social landscape for the better. By being intentional about your relationships and the environments you place yourself in, you can harness the power of social influence to cultivate habits that enrich your life. Start today with minor changes — perhaps initiate conversations about your goals with friends or seek a new group that resonates with your desired habits.

Creating a Supportive Environment
A supportive environment plays a crucial role in building and maintaining habits. When your surroundings nurture rather than hinder your efforts, you set yourself up for success. This concept is rooted in psychology, highlighting how our environment shapes behaviour and influences our ability to stick to new routines. For example, if you're trying to eat healthier, having nutritious foods visible and easily accessible in your kitchen can encourage you to make better food choices. Conversely, if junk food dominates your pantry, the temptation can derail your efforts. Understanding the significance of your environment means recognizing that small changes can lead to significant results. When you consciously design spaces that align with your goals, you create an implicit support system that continually reinforces the habits you want to cultivate. To maximize the effectiveness of your supportive environment, involve others where possible. Share your goals with friends and family who can offer encouragement and create a social context that reinforces your habits. Joining a group can amplify your commitment and provide a sense of accountability. Remember, the people and things you surround yourself with can exponentially influence your mindset and behaviour. By being

aware of these influences and making deliberate choices about your environment, you can create a space that fosters growth and nurtures your journey toward lasting change. Take that step today: identify one small change you can implement in your environment that aligns with your goals, and watch how it can transform your habits.

OVERCOMING BARRIERS TO CHANGE

Identifying Personal Saboteurs
Recognizing the thoughts and behaviours that sabotage habit change is the first step toward achieving lasting transformation. Often, individuals are unaware of the negative self-talk and ingrained habits that pull them away from their goals. For instance, thoughts such as " I'll never stick to this, or I don't have time " can emerge when trying to adopt a healthier lifestyle. These thoughts create barriers that prevent meaningful action. It's crucial to listen to your inner dialogue and take note of any limiting beliefs that arise. Pay attention to moments of self-doubt, procrastination, or fear of failure; these are indicators that you may be sabotaging your efforts. Furthermore, behaviours like habitual snacking while watching TV or skipping the gym because of tiredness can also be forms of self-sabotage, as they reinforce a cycle of complacency and dissatisfaction.Once these personal saboteurs are identified, assessing how they manifest in daily life becomes essential. Observing patterns in your actions and reactions can unveil the hidden triggers that lead to self-defeating behaviours. For example, do you reach for junk food after a long day at work? This may indicate a coping mechanism for stress rather than genuine hunger. Journaling can serve as a practical strategy to articulate your thoughts and feelings, enabling you to pinpoint the moments when self-sabotage occurs. To counteract these negative influences, it's beneficial to devise clear strategies. Establish a routine that incorporates positive affirmations to

combat negative thoughts. Replace self-doubt with empowering statements, such as "I can change" or "I deserve to pursue my goals." Mindfulness can help create space between your thoughts and reactions, allowing you to make more conscious choices rather than falling into old, damaging patterns.Proactively identifying and addressing personal saboteurs is a powerful way to reclaim your journey toward growth. Each small step to acknowledge and redirect negative thoughts empowers you to foster a mindset conducive to change. Embracing the idea that setbacks are a natural part of the process can lessen the emotional weight you assign to them. Consider creating a supportive environment that nurtures healthy habits, such as surrounding yourself with encouraging people or setting up reminders that keep your goals top of mind. A practical tip is to visualize your ideal outcome regularly; this will strengthen your resolve and keep your focus on the goals you wish to achieve. Regular reflection on your successes and challenges provides clarity and reinforces your commitment to unmasking and overcoming the saboteurs in your life.

Developing Resilience and Grit
Resilience and grit are crucial for anyone looking to change their habits effectively. Resilience refers to the ability to bounce back from setbacks, while grit embodies the passion and perseverance needed to achieve long-term goals. Understanding these concepts can make a significant difference when striving to cultivate or break new habits. Resilience allows individuals to navigate challenges and maintain progress despite possible obstacles. Meanwhile, grit fuels the determination necessary to stay the course, even when immediate results are not evident. Together, they create a powerful mindset that keeps you engaged in the change process, promoting a belief that you can overcome difficulties and succeed in your objectives.Building resilience often starts with a mindset shift. Acknowledge that challenges are a natural part of growth. When faced with difficulty, instead of viewing it as a barrier, see it as an opportunity to learn and

strengthen your resolve. Taking a step back to reflect on past experiences can also be enlightening. Recall moments when you faced obstacles and how you managed to overcome them. This reflection reinforces your capacity to handle future challenges and can serve as a motivating reminder of your strength. Mindfulness and stress management techniques can also bolster your resilience, helping you maintain calm and focus in trying times.To enhance your grit, setting specific, achievable goals is crucial. Break down significant goals into smaller, manageable tasks, and celebrate each small victory. This approach nurtures a sense of accomplishment and builds momentum towards larger objectives. Additionally, surrounding yourself with a supportive network can help you remain motivated and focused. Engage with like-minded individuals who encourage your progress and challenge you to persevere. Establishing routines that incorporate these strategies will further solidify your resilience and grit. Embrace the mindset that perseverance is key to habit change. Remember, the journey toward change is often non-linear, and persistence is vital for success.

Strategies for Managing Setbacks

Setbacks are an inevitable part of any habit journey. Recognizing this is the first step toward developing effective strategies to manage them. A proactive approach helps minimize the psychological distress that often accompanies failure. One effective strategy is to maintain a growth mindset. Embrace the belief that challenges are opportunities for learning rather than insurmountable obstacles. This shift in perspective allows you to view setbacks as temporary hurdles that can teach you valuable lessons about resilience and determination. Keeping a journal dedicated to your habit journey can also be quite beneficial. Documenting your successes and struggles can provide insight into patterns that might lead to recurring setbacks. Reflecting on these entries helps you identify triggers and develop tailored responses that keep you on track. It can also be helpful to regularly remind yourself why you started the journey in the first place, as this can reignite your motivation when encountering roadblocks. Creating contingency plans is another crucial aspect of staying on track when facing obstacles. Contingency plans act as safety nets to ensure your progress doesn't completely halt. Begin by anticipating potential setbacks. For instance, if you aim to exercise daily, consider what will happen during days when your schedule is tight or when unexpected events arise. Instead of allowing these circumstances to derail your habit, plan alternative actions. This could include shorter workouts or incorporating physical activities into your existing routines. Collaborating with a buddy can also strengthen your commitment; having a partner can help keep you accountable and provide emotional support during challenging times. Additionally, consider setting up checkpoints or rewards for yourself. Establish small milestones that allow you to celebrate progress, reinforcing your commitment to your ultimate goals. Acknowledge that setbacks provide valuable information on what adjustments are necessary for the future. This mindset encourages adaptability and a willingness to recalibrate your approach rather than surrender to failure. Ultimately, managing setbacks is about resilience and strategy. Each setback can serve as a learning experience, paving the way for more incredible personal growth. One practical tip is to develop a mantra or affirmation to repeat to yourself during tough times. For example, "Setbacks are part of my journey, and I will overcome them." You can navigate challenges with greater confidence and ease by cultivating a proactive mindset and being prepared with contingency plans.

THE ROLE OF MINDFULNESS IN HABIT FORMATION

Understanding Mindfulness

Mindfulness is maintaining a moment-by-moment awareness of our thoughts, feelings, bodily sensations, and surrounding environment. It's a mental state achieved by focusing on the present moment while calmly acknowledging and accepting one's feelings, thoughts, and bodily sensations. This concept is highly relevant to habit formation as it enables individuals to recognize the automatic behaviours that often drive their daily lives. Practising mindfulness, people can identify triggers and patterns associated with their habits. This awareness allows for informed decision-making, making enacting changes and replacing unhelpful habits with healthier ones easier. When we bring our attention to the present, we can understand why we engage in certain behaviours, creating a space between impulse and action crucial for effective habit change.Being present in the moment has numerous benefits that enhance habit effectiveness. When we cultivate mindfulness, we learn to engage with our current experience rather than getting lost in the distractions of our thoughts or the busyness of our environment. This state of awareness not only sharpens our focus but also makes us more attuned to the choices we make throughout the day. When applying mindfulness to habit formation, we can better notice how we feel before, during, and after engaging in a particular habit. This reflection can reveal much about whether a habit serves us well or leads to adverse outcomes, thus motivating us to make conscious adjustments. Furthermore, being present can reduce stress and anxiety, which often derail our efforts to establish healthy habits. This reduction creates a more conducive environment for positive habits to flourish.Consider practising a few moments each day to integrate mindfulness into your routine effectively. Try mindful breathing techniques, focusing solely on your breath and letting go of other thoughts. Alternatively, you could engage in daily activities cautiously, such as eating or walking, being fully aware of each sensation. This practice enhances your ability to remain present and empowers you to recognize the moments when habits occur. Developing this awareness will enable you to assess the effectiveness of your habits and make better choices moving forward, ensuring that they align with your goals for personal growth.

Mindfulness Techniques for Better Awareness
Learning specific mindfulness techniques is fundamental for enhancing self-awareness. One effective method is the body scan, where you systematically focus on different body parts, noticing any sensations without judgment. This practice helps you connect with your physical self and understand how emotions manifest in the body. Another technique is mindful breathing. Concentrating on your breath and noticing each inhalation and exhalation creates an anchor point that calms the mind and broadens your awareness of the present moment. Try setting aside a few minutes daily to practice this. Journaling can also significantly improve self-awareness. By writing down your thoughts and feelings, you clarify your internal dialogue, recognize patterns in your behaviour, and heighten your understanding of your triggers. These techniques work synergistically to deepen your self-awareness, offering a clearer perspective on your thoughts, emotions, and actions.Practising mindfulness methods can significantly aid in gaining control over habits. One approach is the technique of noting. When you engage

in habitual action, pause and label it—such as eating, scrolling, or snapping. This process creates awareness, allowing you to step back and choose whether to continue or redirect your behaviour. Another method involves setting intentions before performing a habit. For instance, if you tend to reach for your phone out of habit, set a clear intention like I choose to focus on my work for the next hour. This reinforces mindfulness and strengthens your resolve to resist automatic behaviours. Regular practice of these techniques cultivates a greater sense of control. Eventually, you may find yourself responding more thoughtfully rather than reacting impulsively, fostering positive changes in your daily routines.Incorporating mindfulness into your daily life can transform your relationship with your thoughts and behaviours. Start with small, manageable practices, and gradually expand as you become more comfortable. The key to effectiveness lies in consistency and patience, allowing the techniques to resonate deeply within your daily activities. Integrating these practices empowers you to navigate life's challenges with increased awareness and control. Remember that every moment offers a new opportunity to be present.

Incorporating Mindfulness into Daily Routines
Weaving mindfulness into your daily habits can be a transformative experience. Start by paying attention to the straightforward, everyday activities you engage in. For instance, when brushing your teeth, focus on the toothbrush's sensations and the toothpaste's taste. Notice how your hand moves, the sound of bristles, and the rhythm of your breathing. Bringing awareness to these small routines can create a ripple effect throughout your day. When you eat, take a moment to appreciate your food's colours, textures, and flavours. Savour each bite slowly, chewing thoroughly and appreciating the nourishment your meal provides. This practice enhances your relationship with food and encourages a deeper connection to the present moment.Creating a habitual practice of mindfulness involves consistency and intention. Identify specific times during the day

when you can dedicate a few moments to mindfulness. This could be during your morning coffee, walking, or sleeping. Set reminders on your phone or incorporate mindfulness prompts into your existing routines. For example, for a few minutes after settling into bed, breathe deeply, reflect on your day, and express gratitude for your experiences. The key is to approach these moments with curiosity and openness. Over time, these minor adjustments can lead to lasting change, helping you develop a more mindful way of living and reacting to stressors in your daily life. Remember, every moment is an opportunity to practice mindfulness, so embrace it wholeheartedly.To truly integrate mindfulness into your life, start each day with a mindful intention. Whether it's committing to being present in conversations or choosing to respond thoughtfully in challenging situations, setting intentions can guide your practice. Remember that mindfulness is not about perfection; it's about being aware and accepting what each moment brings. As you practice, notice changes in your thoughts, feelings, and interactions with the world around you. Allow these observations to influence your daily choices, fostering a more profound sense of connection to yourself and others. In time, this continuous practice will cultivate a rich tapestry of mindfulness woven seamlessly into the fabric of your day.

TECHNOLOGY AND HABITS

The Role of Apps in Habit Tracking
Various apps designed for habit tracking have gained popularity in recent years, and research indicates that they can significantly enhance an individual's ability to form and maintain new habits. One of the reasons these apps are practical is due to their convenience and accessibility. Users can track their habits daily with just a few taps on their phones, making habit formation feel more manageable. Moreover, many apps include reminders and notifications, which can nudge users to stay on track. Studies show that people who utilize habit-tracking apps often experience a higher success rate in reaching their goals, as they provide visual representations of progress, such as graphs and streaks, which can be incredibly motivating. Additionally, community features within some apps allow users to connect, share achievements, and provide mutual support, fostering a sense of accountability crucial for developing lasting habits.Not all habit-tracking apps are created equal, and certain features play a pivotal role in their effectiveness. Key features contributing to these apps' success include customizable goals, user-friendly interfaces, and the ability to track multiple habits at once. Personalizing goals allows users to tailor their tracking experience according to their unique needs and circumstances, making the process more relevant and engaging. Furthermore, a clean and intuitive design can significantly enhance user experience, reducing the likelihood of frustration or abandonment. Tracking multiple habits

simultaneously enhances overall effectiveness by providing users with a more comprehensive view of their progress, leading to a greater understanding of their behaviour patterns. Additionally, many successful apps incorporate elements of gamification, where users earn rewards or badges for reaching milestones, making the process enjoyable and encouraging continued engagement.For anyone interested in enhancing their habit-tracking experience, it's beneficial to experiment with different apps to find one that aligns with personal preferences and goals. Please note which features resonate most, such as journaling capabilities or social sharing aspects, and consider integrating them into daily routines. Deciding on realistic goals, rather than overwhelming oneself with a long list of habits to track, can also increase the likelihood of success. Implementing a strategy of starting small allows users to build confidence and momentum over time. Finally, regularly reflecting on progress will help adjust habits and cultivate a deeper understanding of personal behaviour, leading to sustainable habit formation.

Digital Distractions and Habit Formation

Digital distractions can severely undermine our success in forming and maintaining habits. The constant influx of notifications from apps and social media can fragment our attention, making it nearly impossible to focus on the essential tasks for habit formation. For instance, when you sit down to read a book or write an article, the itch to check your phone can distract you from your intended activity, disrupting your flow. Studies show that each time you get distracted, it can take several minutes to regain focus, stifling progress and discouraging consistency. These interruptions break your concentration and can lead to frustration or inadequacy, especially when you don't meet your expectations regarding habit development.To minimize online distractions and foster the formation of positive habits, it's essential to create a supportive digital environment. One effective strategy is to establish specific times for checking your devices. You can maintain focus during critical periods by setting designated intervals where you allow yourself to engage with social media or emails. Additionally, consider using apps that promote productivity by blocking distracting sites during work hours. Adjusting your notification settings is crucial; turning off non-essential alerts can prevent interruptions derailing your focus. If possible, creating a physical workspace free of digital devices encourages immersion in your tasks, allowing you to develop habits without the continual tug of digital chaos. Another practical method involves using the Pomodoro Technique, where you work in bursts of focused time followed by short breaks. This structure helps in conditioning your brain to associate productivity with dedicated periods, facilitating better habit formation.Establishing a rhythm in your daily routine is vital for overcoming digital distractions. Integrating mindfulness techniques, such as short meditation sessions before you embark on habit-forming tasks, can enhance your concentration. Moreover, reflecting on your accomplishments at the end of each day helps reinforce the habits you are trying to form, making them feel more rewarding. In a fast-paced digital world, assessing your progress allows you to appreciate the small victories. Consider keeping a journal to document your journey; this can serve as a motivation boost and a tracking tool to identify the most challenging distractions and how to tackle them effectively.

Using Technology to Foster Positive Habits

Technology is a powerful ally in developing and reinforcing good habits. With the right tools and applications, anyone can find support in their journey toward more positive behaviours. For instance, habit-tracking apps make it easy to visualize your progress over time. These tools can help you stay accountable by providing reminders and motivating statistics. Daily check-ins and notifications encourage consistency, making those positive habits a part of your daily routine. Moreover, the social aspect of many platforms allows you to connect with friends or communities who share similar goals, further enhancing your commitment. Whether exercising more, reading daily, or maintaining a healthier diet, technology can bridge the gap between intention and action.Plenty of tools are designed specifically to help you stay motivated on your path to positive change. Some apps gamify your journey, turning tasks into a game where you earn rewards for completing activities. This adds an element of fun to the process, transforming your goals into engaging challenges. Other platforms focus on mindfulness and mental health, offering guided meditations or daily affirmations that help reinforce your commitment to change. Utilizing reminders and setting achievable milestones can bolster your motivation. The key lies in finding the tools that resonate with you, whether using a straightforward calendar app to track your goals or diving into more feature-rich applications tailored to your habits.Balancing digital engagement with real-life experiences when approaching technology to foster positive habits is crucial. For example, while tracking your workouts digitally, consider the value of group sports or physical activities where you can meet others face-to-face. This hybrid approach can deepen your social connections while enhancing your dedication to developing healthier routines. Remember that the ultimate goal is to create sustainable habits that enhance your life. So explore different technologies, find what suits your needs, and integrate them into your daily routine. A practical tip to consider is to set aside a few minutes each day to review your progress using your chosen tool. This small reflection time can encourage and motivate you toward your goals.

MOTIVATION: INTRINSIC VS. EXTRINSIC

Understanding Intrinsic Motivation

Intrinsic motivation plays a vital role in habit formation and personal growth. It refers to the drive within an individual, encouraging them to engage in activities for their inherent satisfaction rather than for external rewards. When intrinsically motivated, people tend to be more persistent, engaged, and enthusiastic about their pursuits. This type of motivation supports the development of lasting habits, as individuals are not merely chasing temporary goals but are drawn to the joy and fulfilment that the process provides. Understanding intrinsic motivation is essential because it empowers individuals to create habits aligning with their values and interests. For instance, someone might cultivate a passion for reading not because they want to impress others or meet an arbitrary target but because they genuinely enjoy the escape and knowledge it provides. This deeper connection makes it easier to integrate activities into daily life and stick with them long-term.Enhancing intrinsic motivation requires intentional strategies that can be woven into your daily routine. One practical approach is to create a positive environment that fosters curiosity and exploration. Setting aside time for activities that align with your interests can help sustain your enthusiasm. Additionally, embracing a growth mindset can significantly boost intrinsic motivation. This mindset emphasizes the joy of learning and the belief that skills can be developed over time, making challenges less daunting. Incorporating elements of autonomy into your routine can also enhance feelings of intrinsic motivation. When individuals have control over how they engage with their tasks and can choose their methods, they tend to feel more invested. For example, if someone wants to exercise, allowing them to select their preferred activity can lead to greater satisfaction and commitment. Lastly, seeking out social connections with like-minded individuals can inspire motivation through shared experiences and encouragement. A practical tip to further enhance your intrinsic motivation is to set personal goals that reflect your values and interests. Discover what excites you instead of following a routine defined by outside influences. Whether it's exploring a new hobby or dedicating time to a passionate project, the key is to focus on enjoyment and personal satisfaction rather than on end results or external validation. Reflect regularly on your progress and the pleasure you derive from these pursuits, as this will strengthen your intrinsic motivation and solidify enriching and rewarding habits.

The Impact of Extrinsic Rewards

Extrinsic rewards, such as money, trophies, or praise, can motivate individuals to perform tasks they may not otherwise find appealing. These rewards provide a clear incentive, which can lead to increased effort and higher levels of achievement in the short term. For example, in a workplace setting, bonuses tied to performance metrics encourage employees to meet or exceed targets, fostering productivity. However, there are downsides to relying solely on extrinsic rewards. When tasks become associated primarily with external rewards, individuals may lose intrinsic motivation—the internal desire to perform a task for its own sake. This shift can lead to decreased satisfaction and engagement once the extrinsic rewards are removed, potentially resulting in burnout or a decline in performance. Additionally, overemphasizing rewards can trigger unhealthy competition, creating a toxic environment where collaboration and genuine interest in tasks are suppressed.Finding a balance between intrinsic and extrinsic motivators is crucial to creating a sustainable motivational environment. Intrinsic motivation stems from the enjoyment or fulfilment of the task, while extrinsic motivation provides external validation. Encouraging individuals to set personal goals, pursue interests, and engage in rewarding experiences fosters intrinsic motivation. Simultaneously, incorporating extrinsic rewards strategically can enhance motivation without overshadowing the inherent desire to excel. For instance, recognizing an individual's achievements with a simple acknowledgement can reinforce their internal drive while still offering external validation. This balanced approach sustains motivation and cultivates a more engaged and resilient mindset, enabling individuals to remain invested in their pursuits regardless of external outcomes.In practical terms, consider integrating small, meaningful bonuses alongside opportunities for personal growth within any motivational framework. This dual strategy encourages individuals to seek intrinsic satisfaction from their tasks while providing enough external recognition to drive performance. By fostering an environment that values both types of motivation, it's possible to cultivate lasting engagement and fulfilment, making pursuing goals a rewarding journey rather than a mere race for external rewards.

Balancing Both Types of Motivation
Balancing intrinsic and extrinsic motivation requires a thoughtful approach that caters to both aspects. Intrinsic motivation stems from within; it is the enjoyment of the task, the satisfaction from personal growth, or the passion for learning something new. To nurture intrinsic motivation, create an environment that encourages exploration and autonomy. Set goals that resonate with your values and interests, allowing you to engage deeply with your pursuits. Additionally, incorporating mindfulness practices can help you connect with the intrinsic joy of activities, making you more aware of the fulfilment they

bring.On the other hand, extrinsic motivation, which comes from external rewards such as recognition, money, or praise, also has its role. Integrate external rewards in a way that feels natural and not overly forced. For example, acknowledge your achievements but do not let them overshadow the intrinsic joy of the tasks. Using a mix of both motivations can enhance perseverance in challenging situations. Rewarding yourself after reaching a milestone reinforces the behaviour while inviting space to appreciate the journey.The balance between intrinsic and extrinsic motivation is essential for creating lasting habits. When motivations are aligned, you can sustain engagement over a long period. Research shows that relying solely on extrinsic motivation can lead to burnout and decreased overall satisfaction. Conversely, solely depending on intrinsic motivation without external validation can lead to stagnation or a drop in productivity, particularly in tasks that may feel tedious over time. By recognizing how both types of motivation affect your behaviour, you can adapt your strategy to ensure consistency. For instance, if you find your enthusiasm waning, remind yourself of the purpose behind your actions or seek out opportunities for external recognition. This recognition can reinvigorate your passion and make the effort feel worthwhile. Mixing varying feedback forms—considering both the intrinsic rewards of completing a task and the external accolades—helps maintain enthusiasm.To maintain this balance, regularly check in with yourself about what motivates you most. Reflect on your activities and the sources of your motivation. Are you more driven by personal satisfaction, or are external rewards more enticing? This evaluation can guide your approach in real time, allowing you to adapt as needed. Finding the proper equilibrium enables you to engage in behaviours that are not only pleasurable but beneficial for your long-term goals. One practical tip is establishing a reward system for yourself that includes intrinsic and extrinsic elements. Celebrate small wins by treating yourself to something enjoyable while reflecting on how your actions align with your deeper values. This multi-faceted approach reinforces positive behaviours and deepens your satisfaction with the process, setting the stage for sustained motivation and success.

HABIT FORMATION IN DIFFERENT LIFE STAGES

Childhood and Adolescent Habits

Developmental factors, social environments, and individual experiences influence habits formed during childhood and adolescence. In early childhood, habits are often based on imitation and reinforcement. Young children observe the behaviours of their parents, siblings, and peers, using these observations to shape their actions. For instance, if a child sees parents engaging in regular physical activity or preparing healthy meals, they are more likely to adopt similar habits. As children grow into adolescence, they become more autonomous and influenced by peers, critically reevaluating previously established habits. During this period, adolescents seek identity and independence, which can reshape their healthy or unhealthy habits, depending on their influences.Fostering healthy habits in children and teens requires a strategic approach considering their unique developmental stages. Creating a supportive environment is crucial. Parents can encourage physical activity by making it a family affair, such as biking, hiking, or joining sports. Nutrition can also be a family involvement, where children learn to cook healthy meals alongside their parents, promoting awareness of food choices. Moreover, establishing routines can profoundly impact children's perceptions of behaviours. Setting consistent bedtimes can improve sleep habits, while designated homework times can enhance academic performance. In adolescence, encouraging open dialogues about influences, such as the impact of social media and peer pressure, can help teens navigate their choices more effectively. It's essential to model the habits you wish to instil, as children often emulate the behaviours they see.One practical tip for parents and caregivers is to focus on small, manageable changes rather than overwhelming children with drastic lifestyle shifts. For instance, rather than banning junk food entirely, encourage healthier snack alternatives and involve children in selecting these options. Making this a fun and collaborative effort instils a sense of ownership and commitment to healthy choices. Engaging children and teens in discussions about their habits encourages self-reflection and personal accountability, building a foundation for lifelong healthy behaviours.

Adult Habit Formation and Change
Adults face unique challenges in habit formation due to various life circumstances, such as work, family responsibilities, and time constraints. Unlike children, who are often given structured routines, adults must navigate a landscape filled with competing priorities, making establishing and maintaining new habits difficult. Additionally, many adults may have ingrained habits that have formed over the years, creating resistance to change. However, this landscape also presents opportunities. Adults generally possess greater self-awareness and the ability to reflect on their behaviours, which can be harnessed to facilitate habit change. The key lies in understanding the triggers and motivations behind existing habits and recognizing the personal goals that drive the desire for change.Identifying effective strategies for habit change in adults involves a combination of psychological insight and practical application. One effective approach is to use accountability partners, which adds a social dimension to the process. Sharing goals with someone can create a sense of commitment and encouragement. Additionally, incorporating small, manageable steps can help adults gradually

adjust their routines without feeling overwhelmed. For instance, instead of committing to an hour of exercise, starting with ten minutes can make the habit feel less daunting and more achievable. Another tactic is establishing clear cues and rewards; this helps solidify the association between actions and outcomes, fostering a sense of accomplishment. The key is to remain flexible and patient, as change often takes time and persistence.One practical tip for fostering adult habit change is to use visual reminders. Placing items or notes in prominent places can serve as cues that prompt action throughout the day. For instance, if the goal is to drink more water, keeping a filled water bottle in sight can remind an adult to stay hydrated. This subtle environmental change can significantly impact behaviour, making it easier to adopt new habits without intensive mental effort. Reflecting on successes, no matter how small, can reinforce these habits and create a positive feedback loop that encourages continued progress.

Habits in the Elderly Population
Understanding the significance of habit formation in older people is crucial in promoting their well-being. As individuals age, their routines become more established, and certain habits can profoundly affect their physical and mental health. Positive habits, such as regular physical activity, healthy eating, and social engagement, can enhance their quality of life, reduce the risk of chronic diseases, and even improve cognitive function. Conversely, negative habits like sedentary behaviour or poor nutrition can lead to declines in health and overall happiness. Therefore, recognizing the importance of reinforcing good habits is essential for caregivers, family members, and older people themselves. Encouraging the development of positive habits can help older adults maintain a sense of independence and self-efficacy, making them feel more in control of their lives.Promoting positive habits among older adults can involve several practical techniques tailored to their needs and preferences. One effective approach is to set clear, achievable goals

that align with their interests and abilities. For instance, if an older adult enjoys gardening, encouraging them to cultivate a small vegetable plot promotes physical activity and fosters a sense of accomplishment. Another technique is to create predictable routines that seamlessly incorporate healthy behaviours. Reminders such as notes or digital smartphone alerts can help them remember to engage in activities like taking medications on time or participating in social events. Engaging family members or friends can also provide essential support, making it more likely that older adults will stick to their positive habits. The social element can motivate them, making activities enjoyable and less of a chore.Inspiration and motivation can stem from various sources, including personal stories of others who have successfully adopted positive habits later in life. Sharing these narratives can help to diminish feelings of isolation and encourage older adults to reflect on their journeys positively. It's also valuable to allow individuals to experience the benefits of their new habits firsthand. For example, after a few weeks of regular exercise, they might notice improved energy levels or a better mood. Such tangible effects reinforce the habit and instil a belief in their ability to make meaningful changes. A practical tip is to start small; beginning with manageable activities can foster a sense of achievement and pave the way for more significant lifestyle transformations. Every small step counts, leading to healthier outcomes over time.

THE IMPACT OF STRESS ON HABITS

How Stress Influences Behavior

The relationship between stress and behaviour is complex and multifaceted. When individuals experience stress, it activates a series of physiological responses that can significantly alter their behaviours. This often manifests in changes in mood, performance, and decision-making. Under stress, people may act in ways inconsistent with their usual behaviours. For instance, someone who is usually calm and collected may become irritable or short-tempered when faced with overwhelming stress. The brain's response to stress includes the release of hormones such as cortisol and adrenaline, which can impact mental clarity and emotional regulation. Recognizing these shifts is crucial, as they can lead to habitual responses that may not align with one's values or goals. This can create a feedback loop where stress leads to negative behaviours, which in turn heightens stress levels, creating further emotional turmoil.Identifying specific stressors is essential for maintaining healthy habits. Stressors can vary widely from person to person, but familiar sources include financial worries, work-related pressures, relational conflicts, and significant life changes. These stressors can derail positive habits such as exercise, healthy eating, and mindfulness practices. For example, when faced with a tight deadline, an individual might skip their regular workout routine, opting for a fast-food meal for convenience. While seemingly minor, this decision can lead to a downward spiral as the lack of physical activity and poor nutrition further contribute to heightened stress and diminished well-being. It's essential to develop awareness of the stressors affecting you personally to take proactive steps to mitigate their impact. Keeping a stress journal can be an effective tool for tracking specific triggers and their influence on behaviour, enabling you to identify patterns and make more informed choices moving forward.Consider integrating small but meaningful practices into your daily routine to successfully manage stress and its effects on behaviour. Techniques like deep breathing, regular exercise, and a balanced diet can create a buffer against stress and help reinforce positive habits. Establishing a supportive social network is another key element in alleviating anxiety and bolstering healthy behaviours. By engaging in open conversations about stress, whether with friends, family, or a therapist, you can gain insights to cope more effectively and safeguard your well-being. Remaining proactive about these practices will empower you to make choices that align with your goals, even in the face of stress.

Coping Mechanisms and Habit Change
Learning effective coping mechanisms is crucial for mitigating the effects of stress. Stress can appear in many aspects of life and often leads to physical and emotional discomfort. Finding constructive ways to address stress can help you regain control. Simple techniques such as mindfulness and deep breathing can serve as practical tools. Mindfulness meditation allows you to focus your thoughts and reduce anxiety, while deep breathing exercises can calm your nervous system. Awareness of your body and emotions can also empower you to respond to stress rather than react impulsively.Healthy coping strategies alleviate immediate stress and set the foundation for making positive habit changes over time. For instance, regular physical activity has been shown to improve mood and increase resilience against stress, making it easier to adopt new habits such as better eating

or enhanced productivity. You create an environment that fosters long-lasting change when you replace unhealthy coping methods, like emotional eating or procrastination, with healthier options. Gradually integrating new habits becomes more manageable when the strategies you use to cope with stress are practical and supportive.The journey to change habits requires self-compassion and patience. Reflection is critical; acknowledging your triggers and responses can lead to profound insights. Keep a journal to document how your coping mechanisms help you navigate stress and how they correlate with the habits you wish to change. You create a roadmap by tracking your emotions and behaviours, allowing you to visualize progress. Remember, fostering meaningful changes is often about taking small steps consistently rather than seeking instant mastery. A practical way to start is by choosing one stressor in your life and applying a new coping mechanism to see how it influences your overall habits.

Strategies for Stress Management
Managing stress effectively begins with understanding various strategies that can be tailored to individual needs. One practical approach is mindfulness meditation. By focusing on the present moment, this practice helps in calming the mind and reducing anxiety. Taking just a few minutes each day to sit quietly, breathe deeply, and observe your thoughts can significantly affect how you respond to stressors. Another helpful strategy is engaging in regular physical activity. Whether it's a brisk walk, yoga, or dancing, exercise produces endorphins, which act as natural stress relievers.Additionally, incorporating deep breathing exercises can help control physiological responses to stress. Taking slow, deep breaths can help lower your heart rate and calm your nerves when you feel overwhelmed. Journaling is another valuable tool; by writing down your thoughts and feelings, you can process emotions and gain insights that help mitigate stress. Finally, establishing a strong support network is crucial. Sharing your experiences with friends or family can provide comfort and understanding, reducing feelings of isolation.Implementing

these stress management techniques is essential for fostering habit stability. Begin by gradually incorporating one or two strategies into your daily routine. Consistency is key; make a schedule that includes time for mindfulness or exercise, treating it as a non-negotiable appointment. As these practices become habitual, they will naturally fit into your lifestyle, requiring less effort. Tracking your progress can also enhance your commitment. Keeping a journal or using an app to log your activities and feelings can help you see how these changes affect your stress levels. Remember that it's essential to remain patient with yourself during this process. Building new habits takes time, but the more you integrate these techniques into your life, the more resilient you will become against stress. Lastly, be open to experimenting with different strategies and modifying them to suit your preferences, ensuring your approach remains enjoyable and fulfilling.One practical tip for enhancing stress management is to create a stress relief toolkit. This could include soothing items or activities, such as a favourite book, calming music, or a scented candle. Whenever stress hits, you have a go-to collection to draw upon, making engaging in a positive coping mechanism easier than succumbing to stress. This small preparation can significantly improve your overall ability to manage stress effectively.

THE FUTURE OF HABIT RESEARCH

Emerging Trends in Habit Psychology
Recent advancements in the psychology of habits have revealed fascinating insights into how we form, maintain, and alter our behaviours. Researchers are increasingly utilizing technology to explore habit formation, including mobile apps and wearable devices that track behaviours and provide real-time feedback. This data-driven approach has led to a deeper understanding of the cues and rewards that reinforce habits. For example, studies indicate that habits can be shaped by the context in which they occur, showing that changing one's environment can significantly influence the likelihood of engaging in a particular behaviour. Moreover, the integration of behavioural science and neuroscience has paved the way for developing targeted interventions that address the underlying mechanisms of habits, making them more effective and personalized. As we look towards the future, these emerging trends in habit psychology will likely reshape how we create effective strategies for habit formation. The continued evolution of technology will enable a more individualized approach to habit change, where personalized feedback from apps and devices can guide users in establishing routines that align with their specific goals. Additionally, the growing recognition of the role of mindfulness in habit formation suggests that future strategies may incorporate practices that enhance awareness and intentionality in everyday actions. This could lead to more sustainable habit change, where individuals

adopt new behaviours and develop a deeper understanding of their motivations and triggers. Emphasizing the importance of community and social support, future strategies may leverage social networks to foster accountability and encouragement, making habit formation a more communal effort.To apply these insights practically, consider using technology to track your habits and regularly reflect on your progress. Adjust your environment to minimize cues that trigger undesirable habits while amplifying those that encourage positive behaviours. Building a practice of mindfulness can help you become more attuned to your behavioural patterns, allowing you to make deliberate choices that align with your goals. Utilizing social networks for support can also provide a boost, keeping you accountable and connected as you establish your desired habits.

Interdisciplinary Approaches to Habit Formation
Combining different disciplines provides a richer understanding of how habits form and change. For instance, psychology, neuroscience, and sociology each offer unique insights. Psychology helps us grasp the motivations behind our behaviours, neuroscience reveals how habits are wired in our brains, and sociology examines the influence of social structures and norms on individual habits. By integrating these perspectives, we can see the internal mechanisms of habit formation and the external factors that shape our routines. For example, psychological studies on motivation highlight the importance of intrinsic and extrinsic rewards in habit creation. Neuroscience reveals that habits are often automatic responses embedded in our brain's circuitry. Sociology informs us that social support and community dynamics can bolster or hinder habit formation. This multifaceted approach allows for a more comprehensive understanding of habits and can lead to more effective strategies for habit change.Exploring case studies of successful interdisciplinary habit interventions demonstrates the power of this combined knowledge. One such case is a smoking cessation program that included psychologists, medical doctors, and social

workers. This program not only offered behavioural strategies to cope with cravings but also addressed the participant's mental health and provided community support. Participants were more successful in quitting smoking than those who only received traditional medical treatment. Another compelling example is found in wellness initiatives that blend nutrition science, behavioural psychology, and social marketing to promote healthier eating habits. These programs have significantly improved dietary choices across diverse populations by leveraging peer influence, educational workshops, and personalized feedback. These practical interventions show that when multiple disciplines come together, the result is a deeper understanding of habits and actionable strategies that facilitate lasting change.Adopting an interdisciplinary mindset can significantly enhance your approach to forming or changing habits. Rather than relying solely on one method or perspective, consider how combining insights from various fields can lead to more profound changes. For instance, when trying to adopt a new exercise routine, think about the psychological tricks to keep yourself motivated, the physiological aspects of building endurance, and even the environmental elements that make it easier to stay active. Engaging with these different dimensions can provide a more holistic strategy for developing habits that stick.

Predicting Future Habit Changes
Changes in society often prompt shifts in our daily habits. As cultures evolve and new norms emerge, people adapt their behaviours accordingly. For instance, as the global conversation around mental health becomes more prominent, individuals are increasingly prioritizing self-care activities such as meditation, exercise, and healthy eating. This shift reflects not just personal choice but societal recognition of the importance of mental well-being. Furthermore, many professionals are rethinking their daily routines with the rise of remote work. Once a staple of office life, commuting is replaced by more flexible schedules that allow for a mix of focused work, family time, and personal

interests. This trend could lead to more balanced lifestyles and increased productivity as people tailor their environments to meet their professional and individual needs.Technology is evolving at a breakneck pace, and its influence on our habits is profound. As smart devices become integral to daily life, they change how we communicate, shop, and manage our health. For example, wearable technology that tracks fitness and health data encourages individuals to become more conscious of their well-being. Imagine a future where your wearable device monitors your heart rate and suggests when to hydrate, practice mindfulness, and what types of physical activity to pursue based on your lifestyle and goals. This personalization will shift how we view health and fitness, transforming them from mere activities into integrated aspects of our day-to-day lives. Also, the acceleration of online learning platforms is reshaping educational habits. More people will now find it easy to pursue new skills or hobbies from the comfort of their homes, breaking down the traditional barriers to access and instilling a lifelong learning mindset.Both societal and technological shifts highlight the need for individuals to be adaptable and proactive about their habits. Observing these changes can provide insights into future habits, encouraging us to anticipate and embrace them. An actionable tip is regularly assessing your current habits and considering how they might evolve with changing circumstances. Ask yourself what trends resonate with you, and think about how you can incorporate those into your life today. This forward-thinking approach not only prepares you for the future but also enhances your overall well-being in the present.

PRACTICAL STEPS FOR LASTING CHANGE

Creating a Habit Change Plan
Developing a structured plan for habit change requires a thoughtful approach that blends understanding your motivations with clear, actionable steps. Start by defining the specific habit you want to change or adopt. Be as precise as possible; vague goals can lead to ambiguous results. Once you have a clear target, break your goal into smaller, manageable steps. Each small step becomes a micro-habit contributing to the more significant change, making the process less overwhelming. Setting a timeline can also add a sense of urgency and accountability to your efforts.Key elements that should be included in your habit change plan consist of your motivation, triggers, and accountability mechanisms. Begin with your "why." Understanding the deeper reasons for wanting to make a change strengthens your commitment and helps you push through challenges. Identify what cues or triggers lead to the habit you wish to change. Awareness of these triggers allows you to eliminate them or find ways to replace them with positive alternatives. Lastly, accountability is crucial. Consider sharing your goals with a friend, joining a group, or using an app that tracks your progress. Knowing your intentions can reinforce your commitment and provide valuable support.Creating a habit change plan involves not only your actions but also reshaping your mindset. Cultivating a growth mindset helps you view failures as learning opportunities rather than setbacks. As you navigate your journey,

celebrate small victories along the way. Each step forward builds momentum and motivates you to keep going. Remember, habits take time to form, and consistency is key. Stay flexible and adjust your plan as needed, understanding that each person's habit change process is unique.

The Role of Accountability
Having accountability in your habit journey can significantly enhance your chances of success. When you share your goals with someone else, you create a sense of obligation that motivates you to stay committed. This social pressure can be a powerful motivator; knowing someone is aware of your progress encourages you to stick to tasks even when motivation wavers. Furthermore, accountability partners or groups can provide valuable support and encouragement. They can help remind you of your goals during challenging times and celebrate your successes, no matter how small. This sense of community makes the journey less isolating and more manageable. Additionally, accountability helps to track your progress, allowing you to adjust your strategies when necessary. Recognizing patterns, identifying setbacks, and celebrating achievements become more systematic and less daunting when shared with others.Establishing effective accountability systems can be done in various ways. One of the simplest methods is to find an accountability partner who shares similar goals or interests. Set regular check-ins in person, via text, or video calls. During these check-ins, discuss your progress, challenges, and strategies. Another option is joining a group or community focusing on similar habits or goals. Being part of a collective effort can enhance your commitment, as seeing others work toward their goals can be inspiring. Utilizing digital tools can also streamline your accountability efforts. There are numerous apps available that allow you to track your progress and connect with others who have similar objectives.Additionally, setting up a system of rewards can further motivate you. For instance, treat yourself when you hit specific milestones, thus reinforcing positive behaviour. Consider making your goals public

on social media or in your immediate circle. Sharing your commitment amplifies the sense of accountability and can attract support from unexpected places. A helpful tip for enhancing accountability is to document your journey. Keeping a journal of your habits, reflections, and progress serves as a personal record and reinforces your commitments. Writing down thoughts and feelings related to your progress can deepen your understanding of your motivations and hurdles, making it easier to adapt your strategies moving forward. Regularly revisiting your goals and their reasons can rekindle your passion and drive, making accountability a living part of your journey.

Celebrating Progress and Sustaining Habits
Recognizing and celebrating small wins is essential for building motivation. Each step you take towards a goal, no matter how small, deserves acknowledgement. This practice reinforces the behaviours that lead to success and helps to develop a positive mindset. Celebrating progress triggers feelings of accomplishment, which can be a powerful motivator to keep pushing forward. For instance, if you're working on a new exercise routine, celebrating reaching the first week without skipping a session boosts your confidence and keeps you engaged. Focusing on these small victories creates a rhythm of motivation that encourages persistence and resilience, making challenges feel more manageable. Sustaining habits long-term requires commitment and recognition over time. Regularly acknowledging your progress—whether tracking your workouts, keeping a journal, or simply reminding yourself of your achievements—is a reinforcement tool that keeps the habit alive. When you recognize your journey, you build a narrative around your efforts, making it easier to stay on track even when motivation wanes. For example, if you focus on improving your mental health, note how often you practice gratitude or mindfulness techniques each week. This acknowledgement transforms the act into part of your identity, making it less likely for you to abandon those habits. One practical tip for creating a

sustainable habit is to set short-term milestones that lead to a larger goal. By breaking down a project—like writing a book—into daily or weekly targets and celebrating the completion of each milestone, you maintain enthusiasm throughout the process. This approach keeps you motivated and builds momentum that drives you forward, ensuring that your efforts remain consistent and your goals are within reach.

Made in United States
North Haven, CT
02 May 2025